A Dictionary of Word Processing and Printers

A Dictionary of Word Processing and Printers

Philip E. Burton

Garland Publishing, Inc.
New York & London
1985

Library of Congress Cataloging in Publication Data

Burton, Philip E.
  A dictionary of word processing and printers.

  Bibliography: p.
  1. Word processing—Dictionaries.   2. Word processing—Equipment and supplies—Dictionaries.   I. Title.
HF5548.115.B87   1984   652'.5'0321   84-10348
ISBN 0-8240-7291-X

Published by Garland Publishing, Inc.
136 Madison Avenue, New York, New York 10016

Distribution to bookstores by Kampmann and Co., Inc., New York

Printed in the United States of America

15   14   13   12   11   10   9   8   7   6   5   4   3   2   1

To my wife,
Anne

Contents

Preface

This book is a lexicon of the Brave New World of word processing: word processing today spells o-p-p-o-r-t-u-n-i-t-y.

In every country of the world, from America to Zanzibar, businesses are in a transition from the paper-processing offices of today to the information-processing offices of tomorrow. Many companies, institutions, and other organizations are suffering the confusion of converting to the new machines of the computer age without seriously disrupting their daily routine. The isolated desks and equipment of today are giving way to the integrated workstations of tomorrow.

Word processing has revolutionized the way authors work and the writing of articles and books. It is rapidly displacing even the electronic memory typewriter; it has created the new position of word-processing specialist and downgraded the job of the typist.

Word processing has emerged as one of the dominant uses for personal and small-business computers; as the interest in video games wanes, it is also one of the best justifications for a home computer.

What is word processing?

Basically, it is typing a letter, article, or manuscript into a computer's memory and then using its full processing power to edit, automatically print any number of perfect copies, and then store the document for future use. The material is typed on the screen of a CRT, using a video terminal keyboard, instead of a piece of paper. When the composition is satisfactory, a few more keystrokes will cause the computer to type out the document automatically on a printer or typewriter. The work is stored on magnetic-disk files for future reference and reuse.

If you have written drafts by hand or pecked them out on a typewriter, with an eraser and white-out paint nearby, you can fully appreciate the power of electronic erasing, correcting, and cut-and-paste. Sentences and whole paragraphs can be moved from one place to another in the composition; paragraphs are easily brought in from outside files and inserted like magic wherever they are needed. Tabs and margins are set and just as readily reset, justified, and beautified.

A word processor may be a dedicated system devoted entirely to that purpose, or it may be just one of the many programs or tasks of a personal computer.

There is no doubt that word processing is already producing improvements in the quality and quantity of the printed word. The mind is freed from the demands of the mechanics of writing.

Word processing is the cornerstone of the workstation. The workstation is characterized by a computer keyboard and CRT display with full multifunction capability that may include word processing, computer graphics, magnetic disk and tape files, and electronic mail. Essentially the same unit can be used by the executive, the secretary, the word-processing specialist, the accounting people, the marketing department, the technical people, and all the rest. Everybody will not have all the modules and options, but everybody will be communicating with everybody else. The essential difference between the old and the new is the unseen local area network (LAN), which connects the workstation to all the other workstations, to shared system resources (such as high-speed printers, facsimile machines, data bases, records, files, etc.), and then to every place, resource, and facility that can be reached over ordinary telephone lines. Field service engineers, marketing people, management, and all other folks traveling on business will be connected to their offices and laboratories via the portable computer that ties them, wherever they are, into the company's data bases, electronic mail, and available resources.

The key word in the workstation is communication: interdepartment, interoffice, interplant, international.

Why a workstation? The things that soon become apparent to the manager of an office or plant that is populated with an unplanned proliferation of personal and small-business computers are these:

1. There is a lot of duplicate effort going on and a number of redundant data bases.
2. Many benefits would accrue if any computer in the office could communicate with any other computer there.
3. It is difficult and uneconomical to try to connect Apples to IBMs and Commodores or to any other machines, and the biggest roadblock is the required software.

The integrated office with its workstations connected by a local area network is one answer.

There is a natural connection between the office word processor and the typesetting, copying, and printing of books, brochures, and magazines. Word processors can justify right margins and proportionally space characters in a line to "beautify" the printed page. Nonprinting control characters can be included with the printable characters to be transmitted over telephone lines to a phototypesetting system. These functions are sometimes given the generic term "reprographics." This dictionary includes some definitions from these areas.

Word processing involves, or at least touches upon, the areas of computer graphics, reprographics, telecomputing, teleprocessing, local area networking, printer technology, typesetting, and many other disciplines.

With every new technology comes a raft of new words that the pioneers use to describe their particular requirements, results, and problems. I have tried to restrict the words in this dictionary to those that would be of interest to a word-processor user only, leaving the language of the general-purpose computer to my other works. But, in case of doubt about whether to include a word or not, I chose to include it.

As for credits, I do wish to acknowledge the help and support of all those people who contributed in many diverse ways to the creation of this work. I am particularly indebted to my wife, Anne, for her love, patience, and editorial assistance.

This book is dedicated to Mabel, my word processor, who types 200 words per minute, never makes an error, works overtime without pay, doesn't take coffee breaks, loves to work on legal holidays, proofreads her own copy, and corrects my spelling errors. Her printed copy is a joy to see. She doesn't talk much, either.

And gets along with my wife.

How to Use This Book

This book is organized as an alphabetically ordered dictionary, followed by Appendix A: Printers. Appendix B contains Tables of Powers of 2 and Hexadecimal Arithmetic. Because the primary purpose of this book is to inform and explain, it seemed to me that the reader would appreciate having other related terms in one area.

Many of the terms used in any rapidly evolving technology do not have unique definitions; they may be used in different ways in different situations, and the use of a term can differ from one manufacturer to another. I have tried to list all the meanings I have encountered in my work and study.

All definitions that appear in Appendix A are cross-referenced in the main dictionary. I shall probably be chastised by formal lexicographers for listing terms of more than one word alphabetically in the order in which they are used. For example, "source code" appears under the letter S, and it is not cross-referenced as "code, source" under the letter C. (Dictionaries are expensive enough as it is.) For the same reason, terms are defined as concisely as possible for the layman and novice. Many terms are illustrated with figures, particularly in cases in which a picture is worth the proverbial thousand words. Where appropriate, examples are given to clarify a concept or meaning. An abbreviation will appear in alphabetical order, not at the beginning of the listings for its first letter. (A separate and complete listing of abbreviations and acronyms precedes the main text of the dictionary.)

Words that have the same meaning in the computer world and elsewhere usually are not listed. In writing the book and in determining when it was complete, I attempted to "define in clear, easy-to-understand terms all the essential vocabulary the student or layman needs to read and understand today's burgeoning computer literature." I believe the book meets that goal.

Abbreviations
and Acronyms

Abbreviations and acronyms frequently seen in computer literature are listed in alphabetical order and spelled out on the following pages for the convenience of the reader. (An acronym is a pronounceable mnemonic word, such as BASIC for Beginner's All-purpose Symbolic Instructional Code, formed from the initial letters or groups of letters in a set phrase. If you say "Eee Dee Pee," for example, for EDP, Electronic Data Processing, it is merely an abbreviation.)

The more important ones appear in the main text as well, where they are defined or explained. In some cases, the abbreviation (for example, CPU) is better known than the spelled-out term (central processing unit). The abbreviation CPU will, therefore, be found in the main text in alphabetical order, after cps, and again in parentheses after the spelled-out "central processing unit." Most abbreviations for organizations and physical units, such as cps for cycles per second, appear only in the list.

AAES American Association of Engineering Societies
ACCAP autocoder to COBOL conversion-aid program
ACIA Asynchronous Communications Interface Adapter
ACK acknowledge
ACL access control list, appliance computer language
ACLS automatic control and landing system (military)
ACM Association for Computer Machinery
A/D, A-D analog-to-digital
ADAPSO Association of Data-processing Services Organizations
ADC analog-to-digital converter
ADE Ada development environment

ADP   automatic data processing
ADPE   automatic data-processing equipment
AED   automatic engineering design
AFIPS   American Federation of Information Processing
AIC   activity identification code
AIM   avalanche-induced migration
ALGOL   algorithmic language
ALTRAN   algebraic FORTRAN
ALU   arithmetic/logic unit
ANSI   American National Standards Institute
AP   array processor
APL   A Programming Language
APT   automatically programmed tool(s)
ARIEL   automatic retrieval of information electronically
ARPANET   Advanced Research Projects Agency network
ARQ   automatic repeat request
ASA   American Standards Association
ASC   automatic switching center
ASCII   American Standard Code for Information Interchange
ASF   automatic store and forward
ASR   automatic send and receive
ATE   automatic test equipment
AUTODIN   automatic digital network (of the military communications system)

BASIC   Beginner's All-purpose Symbolic Instructional Code
BCD   binary-coded decimal
BCO   binary-coded octal
BEL   bell character
BEMA   Business Equipment Manufacturers Association
BISYNC, BISYNCH   binary synchronous communications
BIT   built-in test
BITE   built-in test equipment
BOC   Bell operating company
BOT   beginning-of-tape mark or marker
BPS   bits per second
BRS   bibliographic retrieval service
BS   backspace character
BSC   binary synchronous communications
BTAM   basic telecommunications access method

CAD   computer-aided design
CADAM   computer-aided design and manufacturing
CAE   computer-aided engineering
CAI   computer-aided instruction
CAM   computer-aided manufacturing

CAT   computer-aided training
CATV   cable television
CAV   constant angular velocity
CCD   charge-coupled device
CDOS   Cromemco Disk Operating System
CED   capacitance electronic disc
CICS   customer information control system
CLV   constant linear velocity
CMOS   complementary metal oxide semiconductor
COBOL   Common Business-Oriented Language
CODASYL   Conference on Data System Languages
CODEC   coder-decoder
COM   computer output on microfilm
CORAL   Computer On-line Real-Time Applications Language
CP   clock pulse
CPE   consumer premises equipment
cps   characters per second, cycles per second
CPM   critical-path method, cards per minute
CP/M   Control Program/Microcomputer
CPU   central processing unit
CR   carriage-return character
CRC   cyclic-redundancy checking
CRCC   cyclic-redundancy-check character
CROM   control read-only memory
CRT   cathode-ray tube
CSG   constructive solid geometry
CSMA/CD   carrier sense multiple access with collision detection

D/A, D-A   digital-to-analog
DAC   digital-to-analog converter
DC   direct current
DCE   data communications equipment
DDA   digitally directed analog, digital differential analyzer
DDE   direct data entry
DDL   data-description language
DDT   dynamic debugging tool
DEL   delete character or key
DES   data encryption standard
DIP   dual-in-line package
DIV   divide operator (PASCAL)
DLE   data-link escape character
DMA   direct memory access
DMM   digital multimeter
DMOS   double-diffused metal oxide semiconductor
DMS   data-management system

DOS   disk operating system
DPI   data-processing installation, dots per inch
DPM   documents per minute, data-processing manager, digital panel meter
DPMA   Data Processing Management Association
DRAM   dynamic random-access memory
DRAW   direct read after write
DRO   destructive readout
DSD   data-structure diagram
DSS   data systems specification
DTE   data-transmitting equipment
DTL   diode transistor logic
DVM   digital voltmeter
DVST   direct-view-storage tube

EAM   electric accounting machines
EAROM   electrically alterable read-only memory
EBCDIC   extended binary-coded-decimal interchange code
EBR   electron beam recording
ECC   error-correction code
ECL   emitter-coupled logic
ECMA   European Computer Manufacturers Association
EDP   electronic data processing
EDPE   electronic data-processing equipment
EDS   exchangeable disk store
EEPROM, EE-PROM   electrically erasable programmable read-only memory
EFT   electronic funds transfer
EM   end-of-medium character
EMI   electromagnetic interference
ENIAC   electronic numerical integrator and calculator
ENQ   inquiry character
EOF   end-of-file character or mark
EOM   end-of-message character
EOR   end-of-run character
EOT   end-of-tape mark, end-of-transmission character
EPROM   erasable programmable read-only memory
EQU   equate assembler directive
EROM   erasable read-only memory
ESC   escape character
ESD   electrostatic discharge
ESDI   enhanced small-disk interface
ETB   end-of-transmission block character
ETP   electrical tough pitch
ETX   end-of-text character

FAMOS   floating-gate avalanche metal oxide semiconductor
FAX   facsimile

FCC   Federal Communications Commission
FDM   frequency division multiplexing
FE   format effector
FEP   front-end processor
FET   field-effect transistor
FF   form-feed character, flip-flop
FFT   fast Fourier transform
FIB   focused ion beam
FIFO   first in, first out
FIPS   federal information-processing standard
FLOPS   floating-point operations per second
FOCAL   Formula Calculation Language
FORTRAN   Formula Translation Language
FPLA   field-programmable logic array
FPOS   floating-point operations per second
FROM   fusible read-only memory
FS   fusible link, file separator
FSK   frequency-shift keying
FSM   finite-state machine
FTS   Federal Telecommunications System

GDP   generalized drawing primitive
GGG   gadolinium-gallium garnet
GIGO   garbage in, garbage out
GKS   Graphics Kernel System
GPIB   general-purpose interface bus
GS   group separator
GSPC   Graphics Standards Planning Committee

HIPO   hierarchy plus input, process, and output
HIT   hobbyist's interchange tape standard
HLL   high-level language
HT   horizontal tabulating character
HUPS   hybrid uninterruptible power supply
Hz   hertz (cycles per second)

IAL   International Algebraic Language
IBG   interblock gap
IC   integrated circuit
ICE   in-circuit emulation
ICP   inventory control point, International Computer Program
IDP   integrated data processing
IEEE   Institute of Electronic and Electrical Engineers
IFIPS   International Federation of Information-Processing Federations
I^{2}L   integrated injection logic
ILS   integrated logistics support, instrument landing system
IMDOS   Imsai Disk Operating System

IMS   information-management system
I/O   input/output
IPL   initial program loader
ips   inches per second, instructions per second
IPSC   information-processing standards for computers
IRG   interrecord gap
IS   information separator
ISAM   indexed sequential-access method
ISO   International Organization for Standardization
ISR   information storage and retrieval
ISSCC   International Solid-State Circuits Conference

JCL   job-control language
JISC   Japanese Industrial Standards Committee

kHz   kilohertz
KIPS   one thousand instructions per second
KSR   keyboard send and receive

LACN   local area communications network
LAN   local area network
LCD   liquid-crystal display
LED   light-emitting diode
LF   line-feed character
LIFO   last in, first out
LISA   local integrated software architecture
LISP   List Processor
LOGO   a programming language for children (not an abbreviation or acronym)
LP   linear programming
LPI   linear programmed instruction, lines per inch
LPM   lines per minute
LRC   longitudinal-redundancy checking
LRCC   longitudinal-redundancy-check character
LSB   least significant bit, least significant byte
LSD   least significant digit
LSI   large-scale integration
LSW   least significant word

mA   milliampere
MB   megabyte
MCC   monitored command code
MCP   message-control program
MFLOPS   million floating point operations per second
MFM   modified-frequency modulation
MIC   management information center

MICR magnetic-ink character recognition
MIPS millions of instructions per second
MIRLAN midrange local area network
MIS management information system
MIT master instruction tape
MMU memory-management unit
MNOS metal nitride oxide semiconductor
modem, MODEM modulator/demodulator
MOS metal oxide semiconductor
MOTEL Motorola/Intel interface bus
MPU microprocessor unit
MSB most significant bit, most significant byte
MSD most significant digit
MSI medium-scale integration
MSW most significant word
MUX multiplexer
mW milliwatt

NAK negative acknowledge character
NAND NOT AND
NAPLPS North American Presentation Level Protocol System
NAU network addressable unit
NAVIC Navy Information Center
NBS National Bureau of Standards
N/C numerical control
NDR nondestructive read
nm nanometer
NMOS n-channel metal oxide semiconductor
NOP no operation
NOR NOT OR
NOVRAM nonvolatile random-access memory
NRZ non-return-to-zero format
NTDS Naval Tactical Data System
NTSC National Television System Committee
NUL null character

OCR optical character recognition
ODT on-line debugging technique
OED optically encoded disk
OEM original equipment manufacturer
OLRT on-line/real time
OPT operating-program tape
ORD optically reflective disk
OS operating system
OTD optically transmissive disk

PAD   packet assembler and disassembler
PBX   private branch exchange
PC   printed circuit, personal computer
·**PCB**   printed-circuit board
PCE   punch-card equipment
PCM   pulse code modulation
PERT   Program Evaluation and Review Technique
pF   picofarad
PI   programmed instruction
PIA   peripheral interface adapter
PIL   precision in-line
PILOT   programmed instruction language or translator
PLA   programmed logic array
PL/I   programming language/I
PL/M   programming language, microprocessor
PL/1   programming language/1
PMIG   programmer's minimal interface to graphics
PMOS, P-MOS   p-channel metal oxide semiconductor
PMW   private microwave
pn   positive/negative
PNX   private network exchange
P+I   proportional plus integral
PPS   pulses per second
PRF   pulse repetition frequency
PROM   programmable read-only memory
PRR   pulse repetion rate
PSK   phase shift keyed
PSW   program-status word
PWB   printed-wiring board

QIC   quarter-inch common interface

RALU   register and arithmetic logic unit
RAM   random-access memory
RF   radio frequency
RFI   radio-frequency interference
RGB   red, green, blue
RJE   remote job entry
RO   receive only, read only
ROM   read-only memory
RPG   report-program generator
RS   record separator, reset/set
RTA   real-time analyzer
RTC   real-time clock
RTL   resistor-transistor logic

RU   are you? character
RUC   reporting-unit code
RUPS   rotating uninterruptible power supply
R/W   read/write
RZ   return-to-zero format

SBC   single-board computer
SCR   silicon-controlled rectifier
SCSI   small-computer systems interface
SDLC   synchronous data-link control
SHF   super high frequency
SI   shift-in character
SIGGRAPH   Special-Interest Group on Graphics
SIP   single in-line package
SLSI   super-large-scale integration
SM   solid modeling
SMAL   symbolic macroinstruction assembly language
SMD   small magnetic disk, small magnetic drive
SNA   system network architecture
SO   shift-out character
SOH   start-of-heading character
SOM   start-of-message character
SOS   silicon-on-sapphire
SP   space character
spool   simultaneous peripheral operations on line
SRQ   service request
SSI   small-scale integration
SUPS   static uninterruptible power supply
SYN   synchronous idle character
SYSGEN   system-generation program

TDM   time-division multiplexing
TPI   tracks per inch
TTL   transistor-transistor logic
TTY   Teletype
TWX   teletypewriter exchange service

UART   universal asynchronous receiver-transmitter
UIC   unit identification code
ULSI   ultra-large-scale integration
UPC   universal product code
UPS   uninterruptible power supply
US   unit separator
USART   universal synchronous and asynchronous receiver-transmitter
USRT   universal synchronous receiver-transmitter
UUT   unit under test

VDF   vacuum display fluoride
VDI   video display input, video display interface, virtual device interface, visual display input
VDM   virtual device metafile
VDP   video display processor, visual display processor
VDT   video display terminal, visual display terminal
VDU   video display unit, visual display unit
VHD   video high-density disk
VHF   very high frequency
VLED   visible light-emitting diode
VLSI   very large-scale integration
VOM   volt ohmmeter milliammeter
VRC   vertical redundancy checking
VSF   voice store and forward
VT   vertical tabulating character
VTVM   vacuum tube voltmeter

WPM   words per minute
WRU   who are you? character

XNOR   exclusive NOR
XOR   exclusive OR

Dictionary

A

absolute value: the value of a given quantity without regard to its sign (i.e., whether positive or negative). Most computer high-level languages have an absolute-value function, ABS(X), that returns the absolute value of the argument X when it executes. *Example:* if $X = -5.05$, ABS $(X) = 5.05$. Synonymous with absolute magnitude.

accent: a mark, such as ', used in printing, handwriting, and typing to indicate a specific sound value, stress, or pitch to distinguish between another word with the same spelling or to help with the pronunciation.

access: 1: the process of obtaining data from storage or putting data into storage. 2: to attempt to retrieve data from or store data in a storage device.

access arm: the part of a disk-storage unit used to hold one or more read/write heads.

access memory: to fetch a word from memory and store it in a CPU register. The time required is called memory access time and is a criterion of computer speed.

access mode: a COBOL programming technique used to obtain a specific record from a file residing in a storage device or to store a specific record in that file.

accuracy: freedom from error, as opposed to precision; the number of significant digits used to express a quantity. *Example:* a five-place error-free sine table is accurate; a seven-place table with errors is more precise but inaccurate.

acoustic coupler: a computer accessory containing a modem for transmitting digital data over ordinary voice-quality telephone lines. After the receiving number is dialed, the telephone handset is placed in cushioned muffs built into the top of the unit. Serial data inputs are converted by the modem into tones that can be sent over the telephone lines. A similar or identical modem on the receiving end changes the tones back into digital data. Personal computers connect to acoustic couplers via RS-232C serial ports.

action prompt: a computer prompt that halts a running program, which will not be resumed until some appropriate indicated action is taken by the operator.

A/D, A-D: analog-to-digital. *See* **A-to-D converter**.

Ada: a candidate to fulfill the desire of the Department of Defense for a universal programming language, at least for the military. Ada's language heritage is largely PASCAL. It is undergoing tests and evaluation that should be completed by the mid-1980s, after which implementation can proceed in earnest. Ada will figure prominently in real-time multitask applications, especially process control. Ada is named after Ada Byron, Lord Byron's daughter, who worked with Charles Babbage and may be the first computer programmer.

ADC: *See* **analog-to-digital converter**.

adapter: any device used to create compatibility between parts, equipments, subsystems, or whole systems; an interfacing unit.

address: 1: a binary word used by a programmer to designate a particular memory location or input/output (I/O) unit. The computer places the word on its address bus, uniquely selecting the desired memory cell or I/O device. 2: a number, name, or label uniquely identifying a location or a device where data are stored.

address bus: the bus lines that transmit addresses between elements of a computer system: the CPU, memory, and peripheral devices. Only one address at a time may be placed on the bus. One unique location is selected and conditioned to send its data to the CPU or receive data from it.

address field: that part of an instruction word format reserved for an address.

address modification: describing the programming technique of changing a data or instruction address as a program runs.

address offset: 1: a number added to a page number to address a memory location within page boundaries. *See* **page**. 2: a number added to the program counter during a branch instruction to determine a memory address relative to the program counter. Also called relative offset or REL (Motorola).

address register: a special register used by the CPU to store an address. It may be in the CPU itself to address memory or in an I/O unit, where it stores the address word unique to that device. The address word is decoded to wake up the device and make it do it's thing.

address space: the number of words or bytes of main memory (RAM and ROM) that can be addressed by the CPU without additional external logic. The Motorola 68000 16-bit microprocessor has an addressing capability of 16,777,216 bytes; 8-bit CPUs are usually limited to 65,536 bytes or less.

address translation: a memory-management technique. Memory addresses generated by the program are treated as logic addresses, to be interpreted or translated into real-world physical memory locations by the memory-management system before the processor sends the memory access request to the memory system.

adhesive tab: a small gummed tab that must be affixed to the largest notch on the bottom of an 8-inch floppy disk before writing or recording can take place. On 5¼ minidisks, the tab must be attached to prevent or inhibit writing to the disk—just the opposite.

administrative support system: a special word processor specifically designed to improve the productivity of an executive user.

AED: automatic engineering design, an MIT-developed extension of the high-level programming language, ALGOL.

ALGOL: algorithmic language, a high-level programming language designed to facilitate the proper writing and documentation of numerical and other algorithms in a nearly standard, essentially machine-independent form. The language was invented to promote clearer communications between individuals, and it remains one of the better (and still surviving) attempts at a universal programming language. ALGOL was developed by international cooperation to obtain a standardized algorithmic language. It is still widely employed in Europe, but its popularity in this country is waning.

ALGOL 68: a newer (1968) version of ALGOL, more powerful than ALGOL 60 but not an extension of it.

algorithm: a procedure made up of mathematical and/or logic operations that achieves a desired result when followed. *Examples:* Booth's algorithm for microprocessor multiplication; Heron's formula for calculating square roots.

algorithmic: describing a problem-solving process that involves use of an algorithm.

algorithmic convergence: the property of an algorithm to arrive at its solution in a finite number of steps.

algorithmic procedure or routine: a procedure or routine that arrives at its solution in a finite number of steps, not by trial and error.

alias: a name, label, or symbol synonymous with a better-known name.

aliasing: a distortion in raster-scan video displays, caused by the interlacing of the two fields per frame.

allocate: 1: to assign absolute memory locations to routines and subroutines, replacing their symbolic addresses used during program development. 2: to assign a block of memory space to a given function or purpose, either in a computer design or in a program.

alphabet: 1: the English alphabet of 26 letters. 2: the set of symbols that comprise a number system. *Example:* 0, 1, 2, 3, 4, 5, 6, 7 is the alphabet of the octal number system.

alphabet code: the representation of alphabet data with a binary code. Most likely, the ASCII code would be used today. *See* **ASCII**.

alphabetic: having characteristics of an alphabet, as opposed to numeric characteristics.

alphabetic sort: a sort operation on a list that results in an ordering of the items in alphabetic order from a to z or vice versa.

alphabetic string: a string containing all alphabet characters, as opposed to strings containing numbers or a mixture of numbers and alphabet characters.

alphagraphic: pertaining to a display of alphanumeric characters; a text display.

alphamerics: synonymous with alphanumerics, the more popular term.

alphanumeric plane: in computer bit-mapped graphics, a memory plane or bit map for an overlay of lettering that should remain stationary while the rest of the picture is in motion. The severe weather symbol on the TV screen is an example of an overlay that would be implemented with an alphanumeric plane by a graphics computer system.

alphanumerics: the 52 upper- and lower-case letters of the English alphabet and the decimal number symbols 0 through 9. Synonymous with alphamerics, an earlier term not widely used today.

ALTRAN: algebraic FORTRAN, a high-level programming language originated and used at Bell Laboratories for symbolic algebraic manipulation.

ALU: arithmetic/logic unit, one of the basic elements of the CPU. It performs the mathematical addition, subtraction, multiplication, and division operations, as well as binary logic operations, such as OR and AND.

ambiguous file reference: a file name that contains a "wild-card" symbol to indicate that the reference is to any file that contains any character in the wild-card symbol location. *Example:* if the asterisk, *, is the wild-card symbol, TEST*.TXT would refer to TEST1.TXT, TEST4.TXT, TESTA.TXT, etc. Be wary of using ambiguous file references when deleting files; you have been warned.

amplifier: an electronic circuit or device that increases the voltage, current, or power of an input signal or isolates one part of a system from another; an interfacing device.

amplitude: the magnitude of a signal.

analog: 1: something having an analogy to something else. 2: a device convenient to use, operate, and study that represents and performs in a similar manner to a larger, more costly, or more complicated system.

analog-to-digital converter: a hardware interface device that converts analog data into digital form. The precision and cost depend on the number of bits in the converter register. Successive-approximation and dual-slope or ramp types are most popular.

analog voltage: a proportional electrical signal that represents another physical quantity (temperature, fluid level, pressure, etc.). Before it can be used by a digital computer, it must be changed to an acceptable digital form in an analog-to-digital converter.

analysis: 1: the breakdown of a problem, operation, or system into its component parts in order to understand it. 2: the process of studying a system or problem to isolate and define its components and to understand their interrelationships.

analyst: 1: a person who defines problems and develops algorithms and procedures for their solution. 2: a person skilled in the definition and development of techniques for solving problems, especially techniques for solutions on a computer.

ancillary equipment: synonymous with peripheral equipment.

AND function: one of the three basic functions of logic. Any logic (Boolean) expression can be constructed using only AND, OR, and NOT functions. The AND rule for two variables states that if A is true and if B is true, then C is true. It may be extended to any number of input variables and is implemented in hardware with AND gate circuits.

AND operation: the process of applying the AND rule. It may be performed with pencil and paper or by a computer AND instruction. *See* **AND function**.

ANSI: American National Standards Institute, an association that develops and maintains American standards for data transmission, programming languages, optical character recognition, computer definitions, magnetic storage media and format, and many other purposes.

answer mode: in a communications link using modems, the operating condition of a modem ready to send or receive data if it receives a telephone call from another modem in the originate mode.

APL: A Programming Language, an easy-to-learn but powerful high-level language (HLL) created by Kenneth Iverson. It is fairly close to FORTRAN and BASIC. APL enthusiasts like it because the large numbers of operators greatly reduce the sizes of programs. "Function" is in APL what "program" is in other languages. A workspace is all the functions and variables the user has created.

APL/360:   a version of APL tailored to the special requirements of the IBM 360 computer.

append: to add something at the end of something. Word processors usually have an "append" feature to jump quickly to the end of a file to add to it.

applications program or software: a generic term for a user's program, that is, a computer program that is not part of the support software supplied by the computer manufacturer to facilitate use of the system. A computer program written to perform a desired function, task, or operation not connected with the programming or operation of the computer itself.

architecture: the internal block-diagram level, organization, capacity of the buses, temporary storage registers, and control elements within a given microprocessor. Microprocessor architectures vary widely, depending on the major markets for which they are designed and on manufacturers' design and fabrication constraints. Selection of the best unit for a particular application requires study of the architecture of each possible choice.

archive: a central file system containing files meant to be accessed by any authorized person on a network.

archiving: the process of storing data files on system compatible media, to make them available to a wide spectrum of users. *See* **archive**.

area fill: in computer graphics, the painting of a closed area with a uniform tint, a crosshatch, etc. Area fill is a generic term for a rectangle fill, a polygon fill, etc. *See* **painting**.

argument: one of the variables that determine the value of a function. The arguments of a function usually are listed in parentheses after the function symbol. *Example:* alpha (time, distance). In the function tan (y/x) both y and x are arguments of the tangent expression.

ARPANET: a computer network set up by Advanced Research Projects Agency of the Department of Defense. This international network allows its members to use the facilities and access the data from dozens of different computers.

array: 1: an arrangement of objects or symbols in a geometric pattern:

```
                                     3
a  b  f  w                          887
                                   39513
y  u  u  p                        1246733
q  l  v  g                       999999999
                                34343434343
i  s  d  r
```

Square array   **Triangular array**

ROMS (read-only memories) and RAMs (random-access memories) are fabricated as arrays of storage cells. 2: in PASCAL, a data structure that may contain many items (called elements) of the same type.

artificial intelligence: the capability of a smart device to perform functions normally associated with human intelligence, such as reasoning, learning, and self-improvement. Related to machine learning.

ASA: American Standards Association, the former name of the American National Standards Institute (ANSI). *See* **ANSI.**

ascender: the part of a lower-case letter that extends above the top of the print characters without ascenders. In point, the letter t has an ascender; p, q, and g have descenders; o, i, and n have neither.

ascending sort: a numerical sort that orders variables in ascending numerical order.

ASCII: American Standard Code for Information Interchange. A 7-bit character code used for serial data transmission between a CPU and its associated I/O devices, such as keyboards, teletypes (TTY), and video terminals (CRTs). The full ASCII code consists of 128 alphanumerics, punctuation marks, and special symbols. See Table 1. A shorter code, called half ASCII, uses only 96 of the 128 symbols. An eighth "parity" bit is added to the seven data bits to form an 8-bit character when the data is transmitted to external peripheral devices.

assembly language: the programming language that uses mnemonic symbols to indicate what each instruction does when executed. The programmer uses it to write a program without having to remember and write the cumbersome binary codes. Later on, the mnemonics make it easy for a reader of the program to follow its logic and understand the role of each instruction in the overall scheme. Assembly language is the source language for an assembler program. It is one level higher than machine language and one level lower than the so-called high-level languages, such as BASIC, FORTRAN, PASCAL, or COBOL. At each ascending level, more of the mechanical processes of producing machine-language object code are assumed by the computer, thereby unloading the programmer.

Examples:

```
LI     0,3          ;Load accumulator 0 with binary 3
ST     0,CELL1      ;Store accumulator 0 at memory cell 1
BOC    Z,HERE       ;If the accumulator contents are 0,
                    ;branch to the program step labeled "HERE."
```

assembly list or listing: the printed sequential listing of assembly-language mnemonics, along with associated addresses and machine language in hex code. A list is an absolute requirement for program debugging.

Table 1
Full ASCII Code[a, b]

Second Hexadecimal Digit

First Hexadecimal Digit	0	1	2	3	4	5	6	7	8	9	A	B	C	D	E	F
0	✳NUL	SOH	STX	ETX	EOT	ENQ	ACK	BEL	BS	HT	LF	VT	FF	CR	CO	SI✳
1	✳DLE	DC1	DC2	DC3	DC4	NAK	SYN	ETB	CAN	EM	SUB	ESC	FS	GS	ES	US✳
2	SP	!	"	#	$	%	&	'	(	)	✳	+	,	-	.	/
3	0	1	2	3	4	5	6	7	8	9	:	;	<	=	>	?
4	@	A	B	C	D	E	F	G	H	I	J	K	L	M	N	O
5	P	Q	R	S	T	U	V	W	X	Y	Z	[	\	]	^	—
6	`	a	b	c	d	e	f	g	h	i	j	k	l	m	n	o
7	p	q	r	s	t	u	v	w	x	y	z	{			}	~	DEL

✳Teletype control characters.

[a] To find the ASCII binary code for a given symbol: (a) Find the symbol on the chart. (b) Read the first hex digit on the same horizontal line at the left edge of chart. (c) Read the second hex digit on the same vertical line at the top of chart. (d) Convert the 2-digit hex number to binary (see **hexadecimal number system**).

[b] To find the symbol for a given binary code: (a) Add a leading zero, if necessary, and convert the 8-bit binary number into the equivalent 2-digit hex code (see **binary-to-hexadecimal conversion**). (b) Find the first hex digit on the left edge of chart. (c) Find the second hex digit at the top of chart. (d) The desired ASCII

assembly program: an assembler, a computer program that translates a source program written in symbolic assembly language into machine-language binary code that a computer can understand.

assembly time: pertaining to events that occur in a source program at the time it is assembled.

assertion: a statement of fact to be tested for truth or falsehood within an algorithm.

assignable function key: a video terminal key that the user may define or specify what it does when pressed, during a particular program or until re-defined later. Synonymous with user-defined key or soft key.

asterisk: the star symbol, * (ASCII 42), used by some computer programming languages, such as BASIC and FORTRAN, to indicate multiplication: $A * B = A \times B$. Two asterisks indicate exponentiation: $A ** 3 = A^3$.

asynchronous: a mode of operation in which data signals between two pieces of digital equipment are not referenced to a common clock frequency. Asynchronous inputs usually are in serial form and arrive unexpectedly at any time during a computer clock period.

asynchronous transmission: data transmissions not in time synchronization with a common system clock. This results in random time intervals between transactions. Also called start/stop transmission.

asynchronous working: (British): asynchronous operation. *See* **asynchronous**.

ATE: automatic test equipment, now microcomputer- or minicomputer-controlled.

A-to-D converter: analog-to-digital converter. Also abbreviated A/D converter, A-D converter, ADC. *See* **analog-to-digital converter**.

attach: (British): to designate a particular peripheral device, such as a magnetic-disk storage unit, for the exclusive use of one program.

attribute: 1: a characteristic property of an entity, such as a computer file. 2: a data element in a data-base structure. 3: a quality or characteristic that may be assigned to a device type. Attributes for a CRT display are underline, inverse video, blinking, half-intensity, etc.

audit trail: the defined step-by-step path through the various operations in a data-processing system from original document to the computer output.

augend: the number to which an addend is added to produce the sum in an arithmetic operation; an addition operand.

autoanswer: a feature of some data communications systems that do not need anyone to pick up the handset or do anything else because the equipment detects and responds automatically to an incoming call.

autodial: a feature of some smart modems that can automatically dial a prestored telephone number of a distination computer or data bank when a user executes a keystroke command or a software program actuates it.

automata: one plural of automaton.

automatic: any operation, feature, characteristic, etc., performed completely without human assistance, action, or intervention. If such aid is partially required, the operation is semiautomatic.

automatic check: pertaining to the function of a software routine or hardware circuit to detect automatically specific errors or malfunctions. Also known as a built-in check. Synonymous with BIT (built-in test) and BITE (built-in test equipment).

automatic expanison: in automatic typesetting, putting extra space between the characters; the opposite is "kerning," pressing them together.

automatic hyphenation: a feature of some word processors, in which the computer decides where to break a word at the end of a printed or typed line and add a hyphen, in accordance with some algorithm.

automatic letter writing: a feature of some word processors that allows the user to select and merge a number of variables (names, addresses, products, salesmen, etc.) from stored archival information to produce original, new, or personalized documents such as letters.

automatic line limit: in some word processors, the number lines per page can be preset. When this limit is reached, the page is automatically recorded, and the page label is incremented.

automatic sheet feeder: a printer attachment that automatically feeds single sheets of paper into the printer, in lieu of continuous rolls or fanfold paper.

automation: 1: the process of making a machine, system, or factory self-operating and self-controlled. 2: the result of such a process.

autoscore: the underlining of a selected field (word, line, phrase, paragraph, etc.) of text by a word processor when the feature is commanded.

auxiliary equipment: synonymous with off-line equipment.

auxiliary store: (British): synonymous with backing store and backing storage (British). A storage with many times the capacity of the main high-speed memory of the CPU and connected to the system bus lines to support it. *Example:* a magnetic-disk memory. Synonymous with bulk storage and secondary memory.

avionic: pertaining to airborne aviation electronic equipment or systems.

backgrounding: refers to a process run in the background.

background print spooler: a software utility that outputs to a line printer (a spooling operation) when the foreground (higher-priority) programs or users do not require the line printer. The printer-spooler program works in the background in batch mode, queuing up printer jobs until the resources are available, and then runs the printer until all jobs are complete.

background processing: the execution of lower-priority computer programs when higher-priority programs are not using system resources. *See* **foreground processing**.

backing store: (British): an on-line storage with many times the capacity of the CPU main memory, but much slower, used to store programs and data not being used. *Example:* a magnetic-tape transport. Synonymous with auxiliary store, backing storage (British), bulk storage, secondary storage.

backslash: the backslash character, \ (ASCII 92), often used as a delimiter.

backspace: a key found on most terminal keyboards. Generally, the backspace key is used to back up the cursor one character space to erase the last character typed. The same key is labeled RUB or DELETE on other keyboards.

backspace character: a control character received by the printer from a controlling computer, causing the printer to backspace one character.

backtrack: to process a list in reverse order. *Examples:* a list in descending numerical order; an alphabetic list from Z to A.

backup: 1: to copy a file redundantly to save the information in case the original is lost or destroyed. If the file is on disk, the backup file should be written on a completely different disk, tape, cassette, or cartridge and stored in a different location for maximum security. The frequency of the backup operation will depend on how rapidly the data is changing, its difficulty of replacement, and its importance. Magnetic-tape transports are commonly used for backup. 2: a redundant copy of a file or disk.

backup programmer: (IBM structured programming) in team operations, a senior-level programmer and analyst who functions in full-spectrum support of the chief programmer at a detailed task level so that he is constantly in position to assume the chief programmer's responsibilities temporarily or permanently.

backward read: a feature of some magnetic-tape units that read data with the tape in reverse motion and transfer the data to their outputs.

balanced error: an error range with all possible values within the range equally probable and its maximum and minimum bounds are equal in value and opposite in sign.

ball-point print head: a printer mechanism that uses a turret to rotate four miniature ball-point pens (red, blue, green, and black) into writing position under computer control. A head controller coordinates horizontal print head movements with the paper-advance mechanism that controls the vertical motion of the paper, much like a pen plotter, to print text characters or graphics, in color or black on white.

band printer: a high-speed printer of fully formed characters mounted on a rotating band. Band printers can output at rates of hundreds of lines per minute.

bar code: a genre of popular printed codes used with optical-character-recognition equipment (easier to show than to tell; see the following figure). Labels similar to the code shown appear on virtually every kind of retail grocery product. It is the grocery industry's universal product code (UPC). The symbols can vary in size and are designed for use with either fixed position scanners or hand-held wands. *See* **OCR wand**.

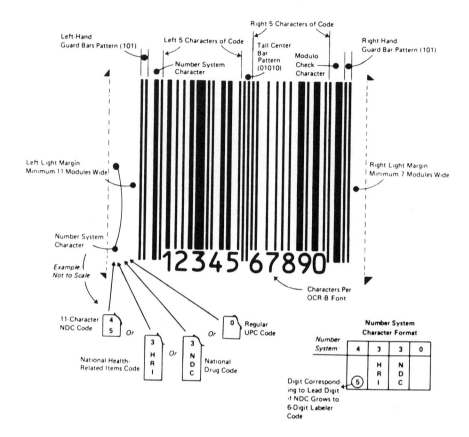

UPC Standard Symbol

bar-code scanner: the electro-optical equipment that reads the familiar black-and-white bar codes printed on most items in retail stores and supermarkets. The scanner converts the printed code into an electrical binary code that can be input to a computer.

bar graph: a common form of computer graphics, particularly useful in presenting business, scientific, or engineering data. Monthly or yearly values of one or more variables are particularly suitable for bar graphs. Quantities for each period are drawn as skinny rectangular tapelike strip areas to be read off against a scale along one side of the chart. See the figure on page 17.

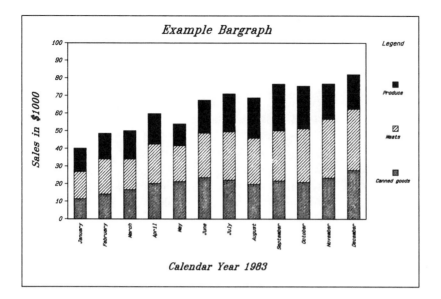

base-aligned: in typesetting, describing anything, such as a rule, that is lined up with the base of a line of type.

Baseline point

baseband modem: a medium-speed (10 Mbits/second, for example), low-bandwidth, limited-distance modem using twisted-pair wiring in local area networks (LANs) for transferring computer data from point to point. *See* **broadband modem.**

base page: the first page of a paged memory, starting at location 0000.

base point: synonymous with radix point.

BASIC: Beginner's All-purpose Symbolic Instructional Code. A high-level programming language particularly suitable for the novice, hobbyist, small businessman, or anyone else who does not need the bookkeeping and mental gymnastics required to program in assembly language to save memory space or cycle time. All personal computers offer a BASIC language interpreter or compiler. BASIC interpreters are available in 8–12K of ROM; extended BASICs with advanced capabilities are available on disk.

batch: input data generated at a previous time and held or stored until a computer is available to process the data, perhaps with similar or like jobs.

batch processing: the processing of input data generated at a previous time and stored until a "batch" is ready or until the computer is available to process the batch, as opposed to real-time processing, in which data are processed at the time they are generated.

battery backup: one way to prevent the loss of data from a volatile semiconductor RAM memory when AC line power is lost or interrupted. A standby battery in parallel with the normal DC supply (derived from the AC line) maintains the proper voltage levels until power is restored.

baud or baud rate: a data communications term, usually synonymous with bits per second, although it does have a more exotic definition for certain complex codes not encountered in microprocessing. A modem operating at 300 baud sends or receives 300 bits per second.

Baudot code: a code for data transmission in which five bits represent one character. It was the code usually employed in many older teleprinter systems. You see it referred to, probably with nostalgia, as "the old five-level Baudot code."

baud rate: synonymous with baud. *See* **baud**.

beautify: a combination command in some word processors. Beautify includes justifying, setting margins, paragraph indenting, etc.

beginning-of-file label: the first record in a file, into which data is written to identify the file and to provide information about its size and how it is organized.

beginning-of-information marker: (British): a rectangle of photoreflective material placed just at the beginning of the usable recording of a magnetic tape, downreel from the physical end of the tape. A beam of light strikes the marker and is reflected into a photodetector, actuating read/write control electronic circuits. Synonymous with beginning-of-tape mark (BOT).

beginning-of-tape mark (BOT): a marker on a magnetic tape used to indicate the beginning of a permissible recording area. *Example:* a photoreflective strip or a transparent section of tape.

benchmark: a test problem or program used to compare computers during selection. The criteria may include speed, throughput, memory space, ease of programming, overall cost, or any other desired characteristic. In surveying, a benchmark is a permanent marker used as a reference point during a survey.

bidirectional: 1: describing a bus line or input/output port on which or through which data is transmitted in either direction. 2: capable of operating in both directions; a bidirectional line printer prints from left to right, drops down a line, and then prints back from right to left.

binary: 1: consisting of, representing, or involving two parts, symbols, or units. 2: the number system with 2 as its base. It has only two symbols: 0 and 1. All modern computers, including microprocessors, use binary numbers and codes within to perform arithmetic and other data processing. A binary number is usually written with the least significant bit (binary digit) on the right. Proceeding to the left, each bit has twice the value of the bit on its right and half the value of the bit on its left. *See* **binary point**.

Decimal	Binary
0	0
1	01
2	10
3	11
4	100
5	101
6	110
7	111
8	1000
9	1001

Example:

Bit value =	64	32	16	8	4	2	1
Decimal 99 =	1	1	0	0	0	1	1

$$(99)_{10} = 64 + 32 + 0 + 0 + 0 + 2 + 1$$

$$= 1\ 1\ 0\ 0\ 0\ 1\ 1$$

where the subscript indicates the base of the number system

binary code: any one of many possible codes that represent numeric, alphabetic, or logical information by groups of binary digits or bits.

binary-coded decimal (BCD): a binary number system or code in which each digit in a decimal number is represented by a 4-bit binary code.

Examples

Decimal	BCD	*Decimal*		*BCD*	
0	0000		1	2	9
1	0001	129	0001	0010	1001
2	0010				
3	0011		3	6	8
4	0100	368	0011	0110	1000
5	0101				
6	0110				
7	0111				
8	1000				
9	1001				

Sometimes the remaining 4-bit binary numbers from 1010 (10) to 1111 (15) are erroneously called BCD. They are not.

binary loader: a start-up program, located in nonvolatile ROM, that contains instructions for loading the full operating system software from disk or cassette. Historically, some binary loaders had to be entered into the computer with front-panel switches whenever power was lost before the computer could read in operating software. Low-cost ROM chips have eliminated this nuisance.

binary notation: the number system with 2 as its base. It has only two symbols, 0 and 1.

binary number: *See* **binary.**

binary operation: 1: an operation with binary operands. 2: an operation involving only two operands.

binary point: the binary number system equivalent of the decimal point. All bits to the left of the binary point are integers in increasing powers of 2; all bits to the right of the binary point are fractions in increasing negative powers of 2.

Position	2^5	2^4	2^3	2^2	2^1	2^0	.	2^{-1}	2^{-2}	2^{-3}		
Weight	32	16	8	4	2	1	.	1/2	1/4	1/8		
			1	0	1	1	.	1	0	1	=	11 5/8

binary representation: synonymous with binary notation.

binary search: a procedure to find an element in an ordered set of data by dividing the set into two halves, one in which the element is known to exist, the other in which it is known not to exist. The latter half is then itself cut into halves in the same way. The process is repeated until the desired element is found. *Example:* the number 76 is to be located by binary search in a one-dimensional array of integers in ascending order from 0 to 100. (British): synonymous with dichotomizing search and binary chop.

binary synchronous communications (BSC, BISYNC, or BISYNCH): a uniform discipline employing a defined set of control characters and control character sequences to transmit synchronously binary-coded data between stations in data communications systems, usually IBM.

binary variable: a variable that can assume only two values, normally 0 and 1.

bind: to translate the intermediate code output of a compiler into executable code by assigning a value to the variable for use in a particular program.

binder: short for binder utility, an operating system program that performs binding.

binder program: a software program that translates an intermediate code output from a compiler into an executable code. Synonymous with binder utility.

binder utility: synonymous with binder program.

binding a program: using a binder utility to translate an intermediate code output from a compiler into an executable code.

binding time: the time at which a variable is assigned a value that can be used in other parts of the program. If the data content of a variable is a result of input data or intermediate calculations, that variable can be bound as soon as its size is definitely determined.

bionic: pertaining to a hardware device that can perform artificially some of the functions of a living system, such as an artificial heart or leg.

bisynchronous: describing an operating mode of a digital communications device, such as a modem, that transmits synchronously in both directions between a sender and receiver. *See* **synchronous transmission.**

bit: a binary digit; the basic element of any binary code, including the binary number system. A bit can have only two possible values, 0 and 1. *See* **binary.**

bit map: a dedicated area of RAM with a 1:1 mapping to each of the picture elements of a video terminal screen or raster. Each bit map is a picture of black-and-white pixels. When several bit planes are "superimposed," varying shades of gray can be created. Color tints can be generated similarly. Synonymous with bit plane and memory plane.

bit packing density: the number of bits recorded per unit of length on a magnetic tape or on one track of a disk, diskette, or minidisk. It is common to have 1600 bits per inch (bpi) using phase-encoding techniques; 6400 bpi is often seen; and even higher packing is possible using special equipment.

blank: the unrecorded part of a tape, disk, or other recording medium.

blank character: a character that will produce a blank or space when transmitted to a printer or CRT. Same as space character.

block: 1: a general term referring to a contiguous group of memory locations, characters, or data. 2: in magnetic recording, a collection of characters, words, or records handled as a single unit.

block copy: synonymous with block transfer.

block diagram: a single plan of a system (mechanical, electronic, computer, etc.) in which the major functional subassemblies (or the functions themselves) are represented by rectangles connected by straight lines. A block diagram is used to show the functional relationships between the component elements and, to some extent, the signal flow.

block header: the first record or records at the beginning of a block of recorded data describing the organization of the file and other pertinent information.

block-ignore character: a character written to a file by the read electronics of a magnetic-tape drive, indicating that a specified block of data has a hard error imbedded in the area of recording and should be rejected during processing.

blocking: describing the process of dividing a record into blocks.

block length: the number of words, records, or characters in a block.

block mark: a character recorded at the end of a variable-length block to mark the end.

block move: in word processors and screen editors, the transfer of a word, line, paragraph, or page from one place in a document to another. The text to be moved is stored temporarily and then inserted in the new location. In some word processors, it may be retrieved and entered more than one time or in more than one place.

block parity: a two-dimensional parity check system capable of detecting and correcting a single error in a transmitted binary message.

Example: The following message was transmitted with even parity in all rows and columns:

```
1 0 1 0 1 0 1 0     1 0 1 0 1 0 1 0
1 1 1 1 1 1 1 1     1 1 1 1 1 1 1 1
0 0 0 0 0 0 0 0     0 0 0 0 0 0 ① 0
1 1 0 0 1 1 0 0     1 1 0 0 1 1 0 0
0 0 1 1 0 0 1 1     0 0 1 1 0 0 1 1
0 0 0 0 1 1 1 1     0 0 0 0 1 1 1 1
1 0 1 0 0 1 0 1     1 0 1 0 0 1 0 1
```
    As transmitted   **As received**

The erroneous bit is easily identified; it causes the even-parity check to fail in both the third row and the seventh column. It is then inverted to correct the received message.

block transfer: the process of moving the contents of contiguous memory locations from one storage area to another. It may be an internal move within semiconductor memory but more often involves an I/O transfer between memory and a peripheral device. DMA transactions generally use block transfers.

bluelines: a preliminary copy of a photo-offset printed page made from the photographic negative before the actual printing run, for proof purposes.

board: 1: a flat piece of material, usually plastic or epoxy, on which electronic components (integrated circuits, transistors, diodes, resistors, capacitors, etc.) are attached and connected together to form some useful circuit; one or more edges may have connector sockets or printed electrical conductors for insertion into a chassis or motherboard. 2: loosely, the circuit mounted on the board. We say that the board is bad, but we mean the circuit, not the board itself. 3: synonymous with card.

boiler plate: in word processing, blocks of text used over and over again, word for word, in different context. Files of boiler plate are maintained and inserted in a work file where needed, using a Read command, which brings in text from an outside file.

boldface: a type font with thick, heavy lines, used for emphasis, in the same way that italics are utilized.

boldfacing: emphasizing certain words, phrases, or sentences by using a **boldface** type.

Boolean: 1: pertaining to the rules of logic formulated by the English mathematician George Boole in 1847. 2: a term used to distinguish a computer logic or expression from an arithmetic expression.

boot: 1: to start up a computer system by using its bootstrap loader routine. 2: short for bootstrap loader. 3: a protective cover that prevents dust, moisture, and other undesirable materials from entering a connector.

BOT: beginning-of-tape. *See* **beginning-of-tape mark**.

bottom-up programming: a building-block approach to programming that starts the program design at the lowest detail module level. Small modules are written to implement defined subfunctions and are then assembled into larger units to perform a specified task. This is the direct opposite of top-down programming, which starts at the top (the root) of the hiercharal tree and leaves the generation of the bottom detail modules until the last. Most program designs are not purely top-down or bottom-up but something in-between.

bottom-up testing: a testing strategy in which the detail modules at the bottom of a system hierarchy are tested first and then integrated into higher-level modules. The opposite is top-down testing.

braces: the symbols { and }, used to enclose automatic typesetting control codes in one automatic typesetting system (Intergraphics).

break: in telecommunications, to interrupt a transmission being received on a channel in order to take control.

broadband modem: a high-speed, high-bandwidth modem used with coaxial cables in a local area network (LAN), handling broadbandwidth services (video, graphics, security, teleconferencing, etc.) or tieing together two or more PBXs (private branch exchanges).

bubble: short for magnetic bubble, a memory technology.

bubble sort: a computer sorting technique that orders lists by successively transposing pairs until a complete ascending or descending sequence is attained.

bufferboard: a printer interface circuit board with a buffer memory to accomodate the difference in the high rate the CPU can output print characters and the slower rate that the printer can use them.

buffered I/O: the use of buffer memories or registers between the CPU and its peripheral devices to facilitate data transfer between units.

buffer-full print: a printer operating mode in which the contents of the print buffer will be automatically printed, followed by a line feed, when a full line of print data (including spaces) has been input and the next data are valid and printable.

buffer memory: 1: one or more buffer registers. A buffer memory may be a section of a computer memory, one or more flip-flops, or shift registers. 2: a memory in which data can be input at one rate and taken out at some other rate, usually slower. A computer outputs characters at a rate much faster than any printer can operate. Some printers have buffer memories that temporarily store characters from the computer until the printer is able to print them. They are then replaced with other characters waiting to be printed.

bug: a problem or error of unknown origin anywhere in computer hardware or software that prevents the system from working properly. The debugging process is the job of finding and eliminating the bug.

built-in test (BIT): self-checking hardware circuits or software program modules that automatically detect certain errors or malfunctions in an equipment and provide some kind of audio or visual indication of failure.

bulk eraser: a magnetic device used to erase completely all data from an entire magnetic tape so that it may be reused. A good bulk eraser will restore the tape to like-new condition with all magnetic domains aligned in the same direction.

bulk erasure: the total erasure of all data stored on any memory medium. *Example:* to reprogram some EPROMs (erasable programmable read-only memory), every cell on the entire chip must be erased simultaneously by exposing the chip to ultraviolet radiation for 15 minutes or more. This is bulk erasure. The newer EEPROMS are byte-erasable.

bulk storage: add-on memory peripheral units capable of storing tens to thousands of times the number of words resident in the computer main semiconductor memory. Bulk-storage capacities are rated in megabytes (1 million bytes). The data stored may be data files, entire programs, or infrequently used subroutines, which can be transferred to and from the internal working memory of the computer as required. Reading or writing from/to these units is slow, compared to semiconductor memory. *Examples:* floppy- and hard-disk drives, magnetic-tape transports, tape-cassette drives.

bullet: in typesetting, the big dot on the left of a line of text to set it off. *Example:*

The three main advantages are:

- Cost
- Reliability
- Short lead time

bundle, bundled, bundling: an increasingly obsolescent business practice of some minicomputer and mainframe computer manufacturers who refuse to sell a hardware computer system without its associated software operating system, utilities, etc., or vice versa. The opposite is unbundled.

bus: 1: a high-current carrying conduct in an electric circuit, used to connect three or more elements, often in the form of a heavy copper bar. 2: in a digital computer, a conductor or a set of parallel conductors that transmits data or addresses between parts of the system. 3: short for bus system.

business analyst, business systems analyst: a person who represents the user's interests during the development and testing of a business computer system. Normally from the business or applications area, he specifies objectives, constraints, and priorities, actively working with other systems people.

byte: in its original usage a byte was defined as eight bits, the length of the ASCII character and half of the typical minicomputer's 16-bit word length. It is sometimes defined as any group of bits having a common function and less than a computer word length. A byte is eight bits—no more, no less.

byte serial: a parallel data-transmission mode in which bytes are sent in serial fashion on a data bus.

C

C: a high-level programming language developed at Bell Labs from the older B language. C is widely used by system programmers and produces a fairly efficient code. Visicorp's VISI ON™ software was written in C, as well as the special effects and graphics in the films *Star Trek II* and *Return of the Jedi.*

cable: one or more electrical wires within a protective sleeve, usually terminated at one or both ends with an electrical connector. If the sleeve consists of or contains a braided jacket of conductive material, such as copper, the cable is shielded.

cache memory: a feature of some of the 32-bit superminicomputers to speed memory access. Data are stored in main semiconductor memory in 8-bit bytes, 16-bit half words, or 32-bit words. Time is saved by fetching these data before they are needed, assembling them when necessary and storing them temporarily in a 32-bit-wide cache register, from which they can be asserted directly on the 32-bit data bus.

CAD: computer-aided design, an automation of the design and drafting process. It is usually associated with massive amounts of memory, a large CRT graphics display, and a light pen—but not necessarily. The term can refer to the calculation of electrical filter design parameters using simple algorithms on a microcomputer.

CAI: computer-aided instruction. Occasionally, one sees the terms computer-assisted or computer-administered instruction, and some prefer computer-aided learning (CAL). There are no rigid definitions of CAI. Any teaching process involving one-on-one interaction between a computer and a student will qualify. The key features: CAI is self-paced (the student progressing at his own pace) and individualized (the student has the undivided attention of the computer, for all practical purposes).

calculator: a small data processor particularly designed for numerical calculations, in general requiring frequent keyboard inputs by a human operator. With some of the new programmable calculators, however, a more accurate description is a small computer with a built-in keyboard.

calligraphic: like or pertaining to calligraphy.

calligraphic-scan: a synonym for vector-scan, a computer graphics technology. *See* **vector; vector graphics**.

calligraphic system: a computer graphics method using stroke technology, in which the computer calculates each path (vector) to be drawn on the CRT screen. The electron beam moves directly from point A to selected point B, instead of horizontally, as in raster-scan methods. Synonymous with stroke graphics and vector-scan. *See* **raster**.

calligraphy: beautiful or elegant handwriting.

camera-ready: describing copy that is perfect, cosmetically, and ready to be photographed for photo-offset printing. The copy must be right because the camera will pick up the slightest flaw or imperfection.

capstan: the rotating spindle or shaft that imparts circular motion to the feed reel of a magnetic-tape transport, cassette, or cartridge drive.

card: 1: a printed-circuit (PC) board on which electronic components (resistors, integrated circuits, capacitors, diodes, etc.) are mounted and interconnected. 2: an obsolescent I/O data-storage medium made of cardboard and punched with holes that can be converted into input data by a computer-controlled peripheral called a card reader. 3: a punch card, sometimes called an IBM card.

caret: in printing and typing, the symbol ∧.

carriage return: the operation that causes the next character to be printed or displayed on a CRT at the first position on the same line. Generally, a carriage return is followed by a line feed, which causes the next character to be printed or displayed in the first position in the following line.

carriage-return character (CR):   a nonprinted control character transmitted by a computer to a printer or a terminal, causing a carriage-return operation.

carriage tape: (British): a synonym for a control or master tape.

carrier sense multiple access with collision detection (CSMA/CD):   the most common local area network interface and protocol standard. Transmission starts only if no other station is transmitting. When transmission begins, a "collision detector" listens in and blocks the transmission of any other station until the network is clear.

cartridge: a container containing a feed reel, a take-up reel, and a length of magnetic tape for reel-to-reel transfer of tape past a read/write head in a cartridge tape transport. The cartridge may or may not contain the capstan or drive mechanism. One of the most popular is the 3M unit, manufactured by the 3M company and others, employing magnetic tape ¼-inch wide.

cassette: a small plastic case containing two reels on which a length of ⅛-inch magnetic tape is wound and rewound. A typical cassette measures 2 inches by 4 inches and is usually nonrepairable, meant to be thrown away. There are two basically different types: digital and audio. Both are used for bulk storage of programs and data when inserted and operated in a cassette tape-transport mechanism under the control of a computer CPU. The cassette is a popular low-cost microcomputer bulk-storage medium.

cassette tape drive: a computer peripheral electromechanical unit that uses low-cost, nonrepairable magnetic-tape cassettes to store computer programs and data.

CAT: computer-aided training, a generic term for almost any use of a computer in education.

catastrophic failure: any failure that renders a component, module, or system totally inoperative.

catena: a chain or connected series; in computing, a chained list or characters in a string.

catenate: (British): to form a catena. Synonymous with concatenate (US).

cathode-ray tube (CRT): an evacuated glass tube containing an electron "gun" that generates a pencillike focused beam of electrons deflected by an electric or magnetic field. The beam strikes a phosphorescent sensitive screen on the face of the tube, causing a visible spot. A CRT is the display element of an oscilloscope, a test instrument that deflects the beam to form patterns used to study the waveforms of electrical signals. A video terminal controls the spot to form alphanumeric characters, graphic symbols, and graphics.

cell: a memory location. Usually, it refers to a register large enough to store an instruction or data word, but it may apply to a single flip-flop storing only one bit.

central processing unit (CPU): the main portion of a computer, usually containing an arithmetic/logic unit (ALU), several temporary storage registers, and a nonvolatile control read-only memory (CROM), interconnected by address, data, and control buses. The microinstructions that implement the computer's instruction set are stored in the CROM. It is better known by its initials, CPU.

central processor: short for central processing unit or CPU.

Centronics interface: the most popular parallel interface for printers. It is a de facto standard, just as the RS-232C is the serial input standard.

certified tape: a special magnetic tape used in the testing of tape-transport mechanisms, particularly the determination of error rates. It is usually an ordinary tape that has been selected for its high quality, with a specified maximum hard-error rate.

chad: pieces of material, usually paper, generated and removed in punching holes in perforated tape or printed paper.

chain: a BASIC-language statement that passes variables from the current program resident in RAM to the next one loaded from a disk. 2: a series or items linked together in some manner. *See* **chained file; daisy chain.**

chained file: a file-handling technique in which each data item or key in a record has the address of another record with the same data or key. If you find one, you've found them all.

chained list: a list in which the items are in several sublists in separate memory locations, but each sublist contains an identifying linkage to the next.

chained program: a program that has linkages inserted in it to call automatically another program.

chained record: a record that has a control field containing the address of the next record in a chain of records scattered randomly throughout the main or secondary memory.

chained search: a search procedure that works like a child's scavenger hunt. Each item found contains an identifier for locating the next item in the search.

chaining search: the same as chained search.

chain printer: a printer in which the links of a revolving chain carry the type slugs.

chain printing: printing out multiple files without operator intervention by chaining the files together. Most word processors cannot chain print without special software. *Example:* MicroPro's popular word-processing program, WordStar, cannot do it without the additional program, Mailmerge.

change dump: a printout to disk or tape of the contents of all main memory locations that have changed since the last dump was made.

channel: 1: a single communications link between a transmitter and a receiver. *Examples:* a wire for serial data; a multiwire bus or cable for parallel information. 2: one of a set of assigned carrier center frequencies within a band of allowed frequencies. 3: the conducting region between the source and drain of a field-effect transistor (FET).

character: a digit, letter of the alphabet, punctuation mark, or other symbol used in representing, organizing, and transmitting data.

character cell: a dot-addressable matrix (e.g., 8 × 10) that can be programmed to display (or print with a suitable printer) a variety of user-designed characters and symbols.

character code: a binary-coded word that represents a character. *Example:* an ASCII character used in transmitting information to or from a video terminal.

character crowding: (British): a data-compression technique in which the space between characters on a magnetic medium is reduced.

character density: the number of characters per unit length or area stored on a medium, as opposed to the bit density.

character height: *See* **point size**.

character fill: to overwrite unwanted or erroneous data in an area of storage with a known specified character to indicate its condition.

character graphics: a graphic image created by printing patterns using one of the standard print characters, such as a period or an asterisk. The computer-drawn Christmas tree at the office a few years ago was a character graphic.

character matrix: the matrix of dots used to print one character with a dot matrix printer. Typical character matrices are 5 × 7 and 7 × 9.

character-oriented: pertaining to any device that is designed to deal with characters rather than bits, bytes, or words.

character reader: a generic term for a device that can detect printed characters, recognize which one it is in a set of allowable characters, and produce a corresponding electrical coded signal input to a digital processor. *Examples:* a magnetic-ink character reader, an optical character reader.

character recognition: the ability of a machine to detect the presence of a written or printed character and express it in a code that can be identified as one of a set of possible or expected characters or symbols.

character set: the total of upper- and lower-case alphabetics, numerals, punctuation marks, and other symbols in the repertoire of a printer mechanism. The sizes and designs of character sets constitute what are called fonts. Synonymous with character repertoire (British).

character string: a sequence of characters to be processed as a group. Synonymous with string.

check character: a character added to a group of transmitted or stored characters and used later to detect errors created during the processing or transmission of the group. Its value is determined by the values of the data characters. See **cyclic-redundancy-check character; longitudinal-redundancy-check character**.

check digit: a nondata digit that serves the same function as a check character.

check indicator: an indicator that shows in some way that a hardware or software check has failed.

checkout routine: synonymous with a debug program.

checkpoint: a point in a computer program at which no calculations or other operations are in process and at which data and preliminary results are in known locations and, therefore, a good point to halt the program to examine its status, correctness, or validity.

checkpoint dump: a dump (printout) of the contents of a portion or all of memory at the instant the program reaches a checkpoint.

check problem: a test problem, with known results, input to test a computer algorithm, program, or hardware. If the computed answer does not agree with the predetermined solution, an error condition exists.

check routine: a software program that performs tests on computers without built-in hardware self-testing.

check sum: the sum of the number of binary ones in a message, character, or word and used later for error detection.

check-sum character: a character added at the end of a block of transmitted data, representing the number of ones in the data block. If the receiving equipment counts the ones and gets a different answer, a transmission error has occurred, either in the data or in the check sum. The block must then be retransmitted.

chrominance: the difference between a color and a chosen reference color of the same luminance, in color TV and color monitors. The chrominance signal is a component of the TV signal, with an amplitude proportional to the desired chrominance.

circuit: 1: in communications, the complete electrical path providing one-way or two-way communication between two points. 2: an interconnection of electronic elements to implement some desired function.

circuit board: short for printed-circuit board. Synonymous with circuit card and PC board.

circuit card: (British): short for printed-circuit card. Synonymous with circuit board and PC board.

circular list: a chained list that returns to the first item on the list when the last item in the sequence is processed.

circumflex: the ASCII up-arrow character or symbol, Λ, sometimes called "hat" or caret (ASCII 94).

clipping: in computer graphics, the deletion of the hidden portions of an object as it is moved around the screen and is obscured by other objects.

close (a window):   in Lisa systems, to remove the window from the display when the associated file is closed.

close a file: to end the reading from and/or writing to a file by calling a subroutine that performs the necessary housekeeping actions.

closed array: an array that cannot be increased in size because to do so would change its total value or its function.

closed loop: 1: a configuration of control electronics in which the output is fed back to the input. *See* **closed-loop control**. 2: a software subroutine that will continue to execute until it is halted by an external action, such as operator intervention.

closed-loop control: the basic principle of feedback servomechanisms and amplifiers; the actual value of the output at any instant is compared with the desired value. Any difference produces an error signal, which is the system input, increasing or decreasing the output until the error is reduced to near zero and the system is stable.

closed routine: a subroutine called from the main program, with a Jump-to-Subroutine instruction and a later Return instruction to the mainline code, back to the next instruction following the call, that is, not an open routine inserted as a block of instructions in the mainline code.

closed subroutine: synonymous with closed routine.

close quote: short for close quotation mark; the one at the right end of a quote.

close statement: an extended BASIC statement that calls the housekeeping routine to close a file for systems with file I/O capability.

cluster: 1: a subdivision of a floppy disk or diskette for housekeeping purposes. One computer system with double-sided, double-density 5¼-inch diskettes has 166 clusters, each with 2048 bytes. A cluster is divided into eight records of 128 bytes. 2: (British): a group of magnetic-medium drive units. 3: a group of terminals and other devices that function as a unit in a multiuser system.

coalesce: literally, to grow together; to combine two or more files into one file. Synonymous with merge, a more popular term.

coaxial cable: an electrical cable that consists of a central conductor surrounded by an insulating dielectric material encased in a braided metallic shield. Usually, a protective insulating outer jacket prevents the cable from causing external short circuits. The metallic shield must be grounded (at one end only to prevent undesirable "ground loops") to minimize electrical noise pickup; that is the primary purpose for using coaxial cable. Coaxial cables are used particularly for transmitting high-frequency signals over relatively short distances.

COBOL: an acronym for Common Business-Oriented Language, the high-level programming language particularly useful in business applications.

CODASYL: Conference on Data System Languages, a committee formed by the Department of Defense to influence the design and standardization of programming languages.

code: 1: a set of unambiguous rules specifying how a group of unique symbols are to be used to represent data or information. 2: the set of unique symbols. 3: to put into the form or symbols of a code; to encode (as in binary, BCD, ASCII, and Morse codes). 4: to write a routine. 5: a code set.

CODEC: a coder-decoder, an integrated circuit that encodes an analog signal into a suitable digital code for transmission over telephone lines and decodes (converts) a digital signal back into its analog form.

code conversion: the translation of one code into another.

coded stop: a halt in a computer program run caused by a stop statement or instruction inserted into the code at a point of interest, usually in the testing and debugging of the program.

code element: one of the unique symbols in the set of symbols for a given code. *Example:* the digit 6 in an octal code or 0 in binary.

code error: synonymous with coding error.

code frame: in digital data transmission, a group of characters that occur periodically in a message. Synonymous with frame.

code key: a control key on a word-processor keyboard. One of two code keys is depressed first, then another letter or symbol that defines the code action. In one system, for example, Code A accesses a sort function, Code H displays a menu of hyphenation mode choices.

coder: 1: a programming technician who takes the flowcharts and other directions from a programmer and converts them into code. 2: anyone who encodes. 3: a digital circuit or device that encodes.

code reading: in structured programming team operations, a "walkthrough" of a code segment by team members.

code redundancy: describing a code that contains check characters or bits in the transmitted data or message, in addition to the information. The check bits or characters are used to detect (error-detection codes) or correct (error-correction codes). One of the many Hamming codes can detect and correct a single error.

coding: 1: the process of writing down the actual code for a source program, usually from some type of flowchart, flow diagram, pseudocode, or other preliminary definition of a program. 2: a listing of computer code for a specific program. 3: synonymous with code.

coding check: an inspection of a coding form or computer listing to find errors and eliminate them.

coding error: an error made in writing a program code, as opposed to an error in the logic. Coding errors are usually due to carelessness. *Example:* in a

National Semiconductor IMP16 assembly-language program, writing LD as the mnemonic for a LOAD IMMEDIATE instruction instead of the correct mnemonic LI.

coding form: a printed form used by some programmers to facilitate the writing and listing of a program code in the proper sequential order for input into a computer. Coding forms provide standardization, convenience, etc. They were more popular when card-punch machines were used for input. Synonymous with coding sheet.

coding line: a single line of code, that is, one instruction in a machine or assembly language or one statement in a high-level language.

coding sheet: synonymous with coding form.

cold boot: a boot initiated at power-on, as opposed to a warm boot executed with the disk operating system already resident in main memory. *See* **boot**.

cold start: synonymous with cold boot.

collate: to combine items from two or more ordered sets into one set having a specified order, not necessarily the same as that of any of the original sets.

collision: in communications, the simultaneous and undesired transmission of two interfering devices on a bus or network.

color: in computer graphics, one of the eight hues that can be created with one of the three primary colors (red, blue, green) or combinations of them.

column: a vertical group of entries in an array or table.

columns of print: the maximum number of characters that can be written in a single printed line by a given printer. Confusing, what? A printed line is, of course, a row. The term originated with the 80-column Hollerith (IBM) card, in which each character to be printed was punched vertically as a number of holes in one column of the card.

combined head: a read/write head for a magnetic-drive unit.

command: 1: a computer instruction intended for immediate action when input, as opposed to an instruction included in a program and executed when the program runs. 2: an instruction to one of the programs that compose the operating system (OS) of a computer to perform a specific action. *Example:* the DELETE command of a text editor. An entire command can consist of the command-name parameters and qualifiers. In the TRS-80 editor, DELETE 100-300 will delete program lines 100-300 when entered.

command chaining: a feature of some operating systems to concatenate commands in a string, separated by some sort of a delimiter. *Example:* in the Data General Eclipse SPEED text editor, the chained command 100L$10K$-10T$10T$$ will move the CRT cursor 100 lines down (100L), kill (erase) 10 lines (10K), and type 10 lines above the cursor (-10T) and 10 lines below the cursor (10T) after the final $$ is entered.

command mode: a computer terminal is in the command mode when no program is running at that terminal and the computer is awaiting a command. In a small computer without disk drive, the ROM monitor is in control.

command procedure: a predefined sequence of commands to be executed by one of the programs of the operating system. Usually, the sequence implements a frequently used action, such as portions of the daily system start-up routine. Command procedures are stored in a file on a magnetic medium and input as required.

comment: the all-important remarks on the right-hand side of a program listing (or written as text between statements). The programmer explains to the reader (including himself later on) what each line of code is supposed to accomplish when the program runs. Comments are necessary parts of program documentation for those languages like BASIC that are not inherently self-documenting.

comment field: the field in an assembler or high-level program listing reserved for comments.

commission: a term left over from the days of the large, multimillion dollar mainframe computer; to insure that a computer has been properly installed and is completely ready for operation. Commissioning may include the running of diagnostic programs or some other form of acceptance tests.

common area: 1: an area of memory containing data tables or utility programs to be used by more than one program or by any user of a multiuser system. 2: an overlay area that may be overwritten at various times by different users or programs.

Common Business-Oriented Language: COBOL's full name. *See* **COBOL**.

common carrier: a public utility company recognized by governing regulatory agencies with jurisdiction as having the right and the responsibility to furnish communication services to the general public. *Examples:* Western Union, the telephone companies, MCI Communications.

common software: (British): a library of modules, subroutines, and whole utility programs with wide applicability in many programs written in the same language.

common storage area: synonymous with common area.

common target machine: (British): a synonym for a target computer. *See* **target computer**.

communication: the passing of information from one person, place, or part of a program to another. Communication may be one-way or two-way.

communications link: the physical way that two remote locations are connected to receive or transmit information to each other.

communications-link controller: a dedicated processor that interfaces a computer to a communications network and relieves it of many protocol chores.

compaction: *See* **data compaction.**

compare: to determine if one datum is equal to another or, in case of numerical quantities, to determine if one is less than, equal to, or greater than another.

compile: to generate machine-language absolute binary object code from a source program written in a high-level language, such as FORTRAN IV. BASIC is usually interpreted, but some computer operating systems support BASIC compilers or semicompilers. The compiling computer produces the machine code only after the entire source code has been entered, although it sometimes requires more than one "pass." An interpreter converts each line of a high-level program as it is encountered at run time; it is much slower and less code efficient.

compile-and-go: (British): describing an operational mode in which a program is loaded, compiled, and executed in one nonstop run.

compile phase: (British): the compile portion of a compile-and-go run.

compiler: a computer program that compiles.

compiler interface: the tasks carried out by an operating system in support of compiler operations.

compiler manager: the portion of a software operating system that controls the compiling of source programs in multiuser systems that compete for system resources.

compiling computer: a reference to a computer that is running a compiler or that is used to compile. A cross-compiler or host computer.

compiling program: a compiler.

complement: 1: the number that is calculated by subtracting a given number from the base or radix of a number system. This is called the radix complement.

Examples: in the decimal system, 10's complement; in binary, 2's complement. 2: the number calculated by subtracting a given number from the largest digit in that number system. *Examples:* in the decimal system, the 9's complement; in binary, the 1's complement. 3: to form the complement of a given number. 4: to invert or negate a digital variable. 5: to cause a flip-flop to toggle or change its output state.

computer: a machine capable of performing mathematical and logic operations on data entered at its input and providing the results as an output in some suitable form.

computer-aided design (CAD):   the increasingly popular applications of the computer for automatic design in automobile styling, logic and electronic circuits, printed-circuit cards, etc. Most programs are highly interactive, many using light pens and expensive high-resolution CRT graphic displays.

computer-aided instruction (CAI):   a burgeoning use for computers at all levels of education. The student interacts with the computer with keyboard and CRT, learning at his own pace (self-paced learning), responding to a pre-programmed course of study. CAI courses can be programmed to lead the student into more difficult material when his responses are correct and into more basic or repeated subject matter when his answers are wrong.

computer jock: a derogatory term applied to a person who is smart enough to use and program computers by one who is not.

computer learning: the process by which some computers can modify a resident program during a run, as a result of periodic or random tests, external events, real-time data inputs, etc.

computer network: one or more computers sharing a common bus system perhaps other resources, and usually having a common purpose.

computer output on microfilm (COM):   a computer-controlled microfilm peripheral that can store data directly on microfilm in vast quantities from mainframe computers. It is too expensive for small-business and personal computer use.

concatenate: to append one string or file to another. ***Example:*** the string "alpha" concatenated to the string "bet" becomes "alphabet." Concatenation is a valuable feature of extended BASIC string handling capabilities. *See* **string**.

condensed mode: a special feature of some of the newer printers with programmable typefaces. The typed characters are squeezed together, in comparison with the normal mode.

Condensed Mode   Normal Mode

conditional hyphen: a hyphen that a word processor inserts in a body of text being formatted, after the operator selects one of several optional hyphenations of the word to be split, as opposed to an unconditional hyphen entered without operator choice.

conditional hyphenation: a word-processing mode in which the computer offers the operator a choice of how a word at the end of a line is to be hyphenated.

conic generation: in vector graphics, firmware generation of circles, arcs, and circles. *See* **vector**.

connective: 1: a logical-operation symbol, such as + or ·. 2: the operation itself, such as OR and AND. ***Examples:*** $A + B$; $A \cdot B$.

connector: 1: a device on the end of an electrical cable of individual wires or attached to a housing or chassis. It provides electrical and mechanical connection of the wires between two cables or between a cable and the chassis. 2: a small circle or other geometric form with a number inside of it on a program flowchart and used to indicate a connection to the symbol with the same number in it, usually on another page of a multiple-page flowchart, but it might be on the same page.

console: 1: the front panel of a computer, containing operating and programming controls, displays, and switches. 2: synonymous with terminal or CRT when they provide the operating and programming controls for a given system.

console switch: a front-panel switch set by an operator to control the computer or input data to it.

constant: a numeric, alphabetic, or string value that never changes during a program run. *Examples:* pi (3.1416), g (32.2), and e (2.7218).

consumables: printer supplies that get used up: paper, ribbons, and ink, mainly.

contention: the competition for the use of shared system resources, such as one of the buses or the printer, by the various elements of a computer system or network.

continuous-feed form: a business form designed for unattended printing by a computer-controlled automatic printer. The paper is in a continuous roll, each individual form separated by perforations for later separation, manually or with a paper burster.

continuous rule: in printers with block graphics capability, a straight line.

control bus: one of the three principal buses of any computer system, along with the data bus and the address bus. The control bus selects and enables memory banks and I/O devices, directs read/write operations, transmitting CPU pulses that control and regulate computer operations.

control character: a nonprinted character in a string of alphanumeric characters inserted to cause a specific control action, such as a line feed (LF), a carriage return (CR), a backspace or rubout on a printer or a CRT. The control character is an ASCII code if the printing characters are ASCII, which is generally the case.

control key: a terminal keyboard key, marked CONTROL, that changes the effect of other keys by generating a control character. The control key is used like the shift key: it is held down while a second alphabetic key is pressed, then both are released. Generally, a control-key sequence causes the computer to execute some specified function. ***Example:*** Control P in my system actuates the printer and causes a printout. Control C logs in a new disk on the disk drive after a warm boot. Control-key sequences may differ in various systems.

control language: *See* **job-control language.**

controller: 1: an interface adapter that enables the CPU to control an I/O unit, such as the floppy-disk controller, a hardware printed-circuit board that controls the operation of the floppy-disk drives for the system. 2: a computer dedicated and programmed for the automatic or semiautomatic control of a process or machine.

control line: an electrical conductor that carries a control pulse, signal, or voltage between two points in a circuit.

control mark: (British): a synonym for a tape mark.

control operation: an action performed by a device, such as the starting or stopping of a particular process. Conventionally, carriage return, line feed, rewind, end-of-transmission, etc., are control operations, whereas the actual reading and transmission of data are not. Synonymous with control function.

control page: in word processing, a page containing a list of special printing instructions.

control panel: the part of a computer console that contains manual controls, indicators, displays, and switches to provide an operator interface, mainly for testing and debugging purposes.

control sequence: 1: two or more control characters typed one after another on a computer keyboard, usually to concatenate a sequence of commands. 2: the normal order of instruction execution; a branch or jump instruction changes the sequence, transferring control to another part of the program.

control signal: a pulse or voltage level transmitted between two devices for control purposes, not for the sending or receiving of data.

control statement: synonymous with declarative statement.

control transfer: a programmed exit from a sequence of instructions that occurs when the CPU responds to a branch or jump instruction.

control-transfer instruction: (British): synonymous with a jump or branch instruction.

control variable: an integer, character, or scalar variable that is assigned an initial value and then counted up or down to control a FOR statement or loop.

convergence: in color graphics, the forming of the cathode-ray tube electron gun's electrons into a narrow pencil beam, using electrostatic deflection plates or magnetic deflection yokes. In color tubes, the three beams (red, blue, and green) must also be aligned parallel to each other.

conversational: synonymous with interactive.

conversational computer: a computer operating in a conversational mode, that is, controlled by an interactive routine, responding with prompts, displays, or messages to operator inputs from the keyboard of a terminal.

conversational CRT: a synonym for a dumb terminal.

conversational mode: a computer operational mode in which man and machine communicate with commands typed from a terminal keyboard and responses displayed on a CRT screen or printer. One of these days it will be done in a true verbal communication between the computer and the operator, using voice recognition and speech synthesis, but for the time being this is still in the development stage. Synonymous with interactive mode.

conversion: the act or result of converting or translating. The most common references are analog-to-digital conversion, digital-to-analog conversion, and code conversion. Short for data conversion.

conversion program: 1: a program that converts data. 2: a program that translates a program written for one computer into a program that will run on a different computer system. 3: a simulator program.

converter: a device or circuit that transforms data from one form or code into another. *Examples:* analog-to-digital converter, digital-to-analog converter, BCD-to-decimal converter, BCD-to-binary converter.

copy: to read data and write it into a new location, leaving the source data unchanged.

copyfitting: the art of estimating how much space a handwritten or typewritten draft copy will occupy when set in type. To do this, you need (1) the width of the line in picas, (2) the number of typeset characters per pica, and (3) the number of characters in the input document.

CORAL: Computer On-line Real-Time Applications Language, a high-level language that facilitates writing programs for real-time applications.

core image file: a file stored on disk, word for word, exactly as it will be loaded into main memory. It is an obsolescent term that originated when magnetic-core main memories were still common.

core memory: an obsolescent computer high-speed main storage device made of tiny magnetic toroid cores that look like little doughnuts, approximately 0.01 inch in diameter. A 1 was stored by saturating the core with magnetic flux in one direction, a 0 by saturating it in the opposite direction. Microcomputers now use semiconductor main memories mostly, instead of magnetic cores, which are slowly disappearing from the scene. Their big advantage was non-volatility of data; if power is lost, the magnetic core retains its stored information indefinitely. But cores are slower and costlier than the semiconductor memories replacing them because more human labor is involved in their fabrication.

Core standard: a de facto computer graphics communications interface standard created by the SIGGRAPH (Special-Interest Group on Graphics) Graphics Standards Planning Committee (GSPC) of the Association for Computer

Machinery (ACM). The Core standard is giving way to the newer Graphics Kernel System (GKS) standard, developed originally by DIN (Deutsches Institut für Normung).

core store: (British): a core memory. *See* **core memory**.

correspondence quality: a descriptive marketing term for a print quality much better than low-cost dot-matrix print characters, and implying some superiority over the fully formed "letter-quality" print of the competition. Synonymous with letter quality, in my book.

corruption (of data): the pollution of data with errors or the possibility of errors as the result of a hardware or software malfunction.

count: 1: an accumulated total of the number of occurrences of a particular event of interest. 2: to keep track of the number of occurrences of a particular event.

counter variable: in a high-level programming language, the variable that keeps track of the number of times a loop is executed. *Example:* in the BASIC statement,

10 FOR I = 1 TO 10

I is the counter variable and will assume values from 1 to 10 as the program runs.

courseware: the software programs, associated manuals, workbooks, and other documentation for computer-assisted instruction.

CP/M: Control Program/Microcomputer, the most widely used microcomputer operating system, is a software development of the Digital Research Corporation. CP/M is their registered trademark. *See* **operating system**.

cps: 1: characters per second, in data transmission. 2: cycles per second, a unit of frequency, now called hertz.

CPU: central processing unit, the major and controlling unit of a digital computer. It contains an arithmetic/logic unit (ALU), a number of special registers, a control read-only memory (CROM), and necessary control circuits. The CPU fetches instructions, decodes and executes them, performs arithmetic, controls the use of memory, and provides timing signals, start-up routines, etc.

CR: the carriage return, a nonprinted control character. When received by a printer or CRT terminal, it causes the print head or cursor to move to the start of the line, at the left margin.

crash: a computer program or a computer is said to crash when the CPU loses control. The program goes amok and generally everything is read/write memory is subject to change without notice. *See* **head crash**.

CRC: *See* **cyclic-redundancy checking**.

CRCC: the cyclic-redundancy-check character. *See* **cyclic-redundancy-check character**; **cyclic-redundancy checking**.

CREATE: a BASIC statement or command that directs the interpreter to create a new file with the name specified by a following file-name argument.

create (a file): to identify to the interpreter or compiler that you wish to start a new file with the name given in a following file-name argument.

crippled mode: (British): a degraded mode of operation when a system runs with reduced or limited capabilities after the failure of one or more parts; a failsoft system (US).

cross: an adjective used to describe a microcomputer support software program that is entered into and runs on a larger host computer, usually a minicomputer. *Example:* Motorola supplies a cross-PASCAL compiler that is input into an IBM 370 host computer to compile source programs written in PASCAL for the MC68000 microprocessor.

cross-assembler: an assembler program for one computer that is loaded into and run on another (usually larger) machine called the host computer. *See* **cross**; **cross-software**.

cross-check: a verification of the result of an operation, particularly a mathematical calculation, by solving the problem with another method and comparing answers.

cross-compiler: a compiler program for one computer that is loaded into and run on another (usually larger) machine called the host computer. *See* **cross**; **cross-software**.

crossfoot: to sum each row of a table horizontally, and each column vertically, in a table of numerical values.

cross-macroassembler: a macroassember for one computer loaded and run on a larger host computer. *See* **cross**.

cross-software: a generic class of software whose members included cross-assemblers and cross-compilers. Cross-software assembles or compiles programs for one computer while running on a larger host computer. The alternative to cross-software is resident software, which assembles or compiles programs using the same type of computer in which the programs will eventually run.

cross-talk: the undesired interference (noise) signals inductively or capacitively coupled into a communications channel, cable, or wire by another adjacent to it.

CRT: cathode-ray tube, the TV-like screen of video monitors, terminals, and oscilloscopes.

CRT controller chip: an LSI chip that supplies CRT control signals for CRT alphanumeric displays.

crunch: (slang): to process. The usual reference is number crunching, the mathematical manipulation of data.

cue: 1: a signal recorded on tape during electronic dictation by the boss to mark significant points or locations for the transcribing person. 2: (British): an instruction that contains a key to initiate entry into a closed subroutine.

current line: the pointer used in an editor routine to keep track of the line being edited within a file. The cursor keeps track of the character being edited within the line.

cursor: a moving, sliding, or blinking symbol on a CRT that indicates where the next character will appear.

cursor key: a keyboard key that positions the cursor on a video monitor (CRT) screen. Most cursor keys are marked with arrows indicating the direction of movement: ↑, ↓, ←, →. The HOME key causes the cursor to move to the upper leftmost position on the screen. Some keys are marked N, S, E, or W for the cardinal compass directions.

cut-and-paste: a word-processing and text-editing capability to mark electronically (cut) and move a block of text to a new location (paste). The term comes from the old scissors-and-glue editing procedure with paper.

cut-sheet feeder: a printer accessory mechanism that automatically feeds cut sheets (for example, the standard 8½-by-11-inch sheets) into an printer under computer control.

cut-sheet paper: paper in the form of a standard 8½-by-11-inch or legal-size sheet, as opposed to such other printer paper forms as continuous roll, fanfold, or tractor-feed.

cycle: 1: once around a circuit. 2: the time interval between periodic, repeating events. 3: a portion of a mechanical programmer or timer period, such as a wash cycle, rinse cycle, etc.

cycles per second (cps): the unit of frequency for a sinusoidal alternating current or voltage, synonymous with hertz: 1 cps = 1 Hz; 1 megacycle per second = 1 megahertz (MHz).

cyclic-redundancy-check character (CRCC): a character used in a modified cyclic code and added to the end of a block of transmitted or recorded data for later detection and correction of errors. *See* **cyclic-redundancy checking**.

cyclic-redundancy checking (CRC): one of the most popular and most effective means of detecting an error in a bit stream of serially transmitted data, such as in data communications and magnetic recording. Each block of data to be transmitted is divided by a constant bit pattern called the generating polynomial (GP). The remainder (not the quotient) is the CRC word, which is appended at the end of the transmitted data. At the receiving end, the data block is also divided by the same GP, and the remainder is compared with the received CRC word. The two must be the same unless an error has occurred. If the two do not agree, the transmission must be repeated. An integrated circuit now on the market performs all the functions of CRC generation and checking, including programmable selection of one of many GPs. GPs are expressed, for example, as $X^{16} + X^{12} + X^5 + X^0$, representing the following 17-bit pattern:

2^{16}	2^{15}	2^{14}	2^{13}	2^{12}	2^{11}	2^{10}	2^9	2^8	2^7	2^6	2^5	2^4	2^3	2^2	2^1	2^0
1	0	0	0	1	0	0	0	0	0	0	1	0	0	0	0	1

D

D/A, D-A: digital-to-analog. *See* **digital-to-analog converter**.

DAC: digital-to-analog converter. Also abbreviated D/A converter, D-A converter. *See* **digital-to-analog converter**.

daisy: short for daisy wheel or daisy-wheel printer.

daisy chain: 1: a bus line interconnecting peripheral units in serial fashion, allowing a CPU interrupt control signal to pass down the chain from the nearest device to the last in line. Daisy chaining is one of the simplest interrupt priority systems. The first to be serviced is physically located next to the CPU; the unit with the lowest priority is farthest from it. 2: to move a signal in a serial mode from one unit to another.

daisy wheel: a print head in the form of a plastic disk with fully formed type characters at the end of arms radiating from the center of the disk, like daisy petals, forming a flat type wheel. On a given daisy wheel, all characters have the same font. But daisy wheels are designed to be interchangeable with other wheels having different typefaces.

(Courtesy of Inmac.)

daisy-wheel printer: a type of printer mechanization that employs a daisy-wheel print head. *See* **daisy wheel.**

Dartmouth BASIC: the standard Beginner's All-purpose Symbolic Instructional Code, the most widely used high-level language, particularly in personal and small-business computers. BASIC was originally developed at Dartmouth.

data: according to Webster's, "factual material used as a basis, especially for discussion and decision, something used for calculating and measuring." Data are pieces of information to be input to a computer, processed in some way, operated on, and output by the computer. The information must be put into a form (format) the computer can understand before it can be input. Similarly, the computer must organize its output data into a form that the output device can understand and assimilate. Although instructions, addresses, and numeric information are all data, some distinction is ordinarily made; computer words are usually called instruction words and data words, the latter referring to the numeric or alphanumeric information to be processed.

data-acquisition system: a system designed to detect, measure, format, record, or store information and transmit it to a remote location where it may be further processed and/or displayed.

data-adapter unit: in communication networks, a unit that interfaces a processor to a data communication channel.

data area: the region of main memory in which data are stored, as opposed to a program area.

data array: *See* **array.**

data attribute: *See* **attribute.**

data bank: a comprehensive collection of data. ***Example:*** one line of an invoice may form an item, a complete invoice may be a record, a complete set of such records may form a file, the collection of inventory control files may form a library, and the libraries used by an organization are called its data bank. Data banks are usually available to many users connected to the storing computer by remote terminals.

data base: 1: a data bank. 2: a collection of data, at least as large as a file, as defined by a particular user or system. 3: a file of interrelated data stored together to serve one or more users. 4: the total set of relevant data available to the computer or its users.

data-base administrator: the person responsible for the quality and integrity of a data base.

data-base designer: the person who developed the structure of the data base and its rules of operation.

data-base manager: a software program for computer systems in which several users access large data bases. The program efficiently stores, updates, and retrieves data items, normally from magnetic-disk files, with a minimum of human interaction, performing the function of data-base management.

data bus: a bus system that interconnects the CPU, memory, and all the peripheral I/O units of a computer system for the purpose of exchanging data.

data carrier: (British): any medium for recording data: floppy disks, magnetic tape, punch cards and tape.

data chaining: a technique for recording data in which parts of a logic record are scattered or distributed in separate parts of a physical record or file but are connected together by an identifier or chaining code that tells the computer where to find the next link in the chain. *See* **physical record**.

data channel: a channel used for the transmission or exchange of data. *See* **channel**.

data collection: 1: the taking of samples or measurements until some criterion is satisfied, usually where a statistically significant quantity of samples has been reached. 2: the act of gathering data at a central point from two or more remote sources.

data communication: the transmission, reception, and validation of data.

data communications equipment (DCE):   units that establish, maintain, and terminate a data link. DCE provides signal conversion and coding required for communication between sender and receiver. This equipment may be an integral part of a computer system, such as a modem.

data compaction: a generic term for any process used to reduce the required parameters of the data: bandwidth, storage space, processing time, etc. *Examples:* the packing of binary-coded decimal digits into 8-bit and 16-bit words, stripping of leading zeros, and elimination of NOP instructions.

data concentration: the collection of data at an intermediate point from several low- and medium-speed communication lines for retransmission over high-speed lines.

data conversion: the translation of signals or data from one form or format into another, such as analog-to-digital or digital-to-analog conversions.

data density: synonymous with bit packing density, a magnetic-disk or -tape term.

data-description language (DDL): a data-base management language used to define the structure and relationships of data elements and records in a particular file.

data dictionary: *See* **dictionary.**

data display unit: a synonym for a video terminal.

data element: 1: a set of data items to be regarded and handled as a unit in a particular application. 2: a unit of data defined in a data dictionary. 3: a field in a record.

data-element chain: two or more data elements in an ordered set used as a single data element.

data encryption: the encoding of data using secret codes to secure the information against unauthorized use.

data format: *See* **format.**

data gathering: a synonym for data collection.

data handling: a general term describing nonarithmetic computer functions, such as searching, sorting, retrieving, comparing, etc.

data highway: an intraplant data bus for distributed control, sometimes made with fiber optics.

data item: one of the units of data describing a particular data attribute in a record.

data link: the communications, lines, modems, and controls of all stations connected to the line used to transmit information between two or more stations.

data management: the control of and provisions for storing, retrieving, modifying, appending, securing, and efficient use of data files in a given computer system.

data-management system: a software system that provides the user with the capability to control, update, augment, move, and otherwise manipulate large data bases stored in a computer. Most data-management programs use a conversational easy-to-use language intended for business people, not EDP professionals.

data manipulation: another term, like data handling, used to describe the nonnumerical computer applications, such as sorting, report generation, printing, etc.

data matrix: an array of string or numerical values. *See* **array**.

data name: a descriptive label assigned by a programmer to a variable, field, or record.

data-path electronics: in a disk drive, the hardware circuits that implement the signal conditioning between the rotating magnetic disk's read/write head and the microcomputer data bus.

data processing: the execution of a systematic sequence of mathematical and/or logical operations performed on data by a computer.

data processor: synonymous with computer.

data purification: manual or semiautomatic preprocessing of computer input data to eliminate as many errors as possible.

data reduction: the processing of raw test measurement results into ordered, smoothed, converted, or more useful items.

data retrieval: copying data from a storage location to a site where it may be used. Usually, it refers to recovery of data by computer from a large bulk-storage unit file where it had been stored earlier, after classification and coding for expeditious retrieval. Synonymous with information retrieval.

data set: 1: in remote communication networks, the electronic black box used to interface a computer with the network. 2: a combination of related data items. 3: a telephone instrument used with a modem, essentially for data transmitting and receiving.

data sink: the receiving end of a data link; the other end is a data source.

data source: the sending end of a data link; the other end is a data sink.

data-structure diagram (DSD): in structured analysis, a graphic tool representing the entities, attributes, and data relationships necessary to retrieve data immediately from a data base in response to an inquiry.

data tablet: a computer graphics input device with a surface area about 1 square foot, with a stylus for drawing figures to be input to a computer. Synonymous with graphics tablet.

data terminal: synonymous with terminal.

data transaction: an operation carried out on data. Synonymous with data processing.

data transmission: 1: the transfer of data from one point to another. 2: the data that was transferred.

data word: a computer word that is data, as opposed to an instruction word.

datum: the singular of data.

DCE port: a data communications equipment port, one of two types of EIA RS-232C serial interface standard ports; the other is the DTE (data terminal equipment) port.

DDL: data-description language, a data-base management system language used to define the structure and relationships of data elements and records in a particular file.

deblocking: the extraction of records from a block of recorded data for processing.

debug: 1: to detect and remove errors from a computer program or hardware. 2: to troubleshoot. 3: the mnemonic name for a software or firmware program that uses a CRT or printer to display the contents of memory locations, accumulator data, and contents of other registers of particular interest to the troubleshooter. A debugging program causes the program to run and then halt at predetermined locations called breakpoints. It prints out the contents of the registers of interest at that time.

decade: a group, set, or series of 10 objects or events. *Examples:* a decade counter that has a modulus of 10, a decade resistor box that inserts resistance between two terminals of a test box in steps of 10.

decimal alignment: the alignment of the decimal points in a column of numbers rather than on the most significant (leftmost) digit. The decimal points line up, but the left-hand margin may be ragged.

decimal notation: the familiar decimal number system.

decimal number system: the number system with 10 as its base or radix, presumably originated by the caveman to indicate quantities with his fingers, the first digits.

decimal point: 1: the radix point in the decimal number system. 2: the point that marks the place in a decimal number between the positive and negative powers of 10 or between the integer part and the fractional part of the number.

decimal tab: a tab that aligns the decimal point in columns of numbers rather than the leftmost characters, as in a normal tab operation. When no decimal point is used, decimal tab can be used to align right-hand margins of columns. Synonymous with align tab.

deck: a set of punched cards. The use of punch cards is decreasing rapidly because of the development of low-cost disk and tape storage devices. A card-punch operator would be well advised to retrain.

decode: 1: to translate a message in code back into the original language in which it was written. 2: to convert one code into another code.

decrement: 1: to decrease in amount. 2: the amount lost by reduction. 3: a negative increment.

default: 1: failure to perform a required or expected act. 2: describing a value that will be used in a computer program unless another value is input to replace it.

default action: a predefined action taken by the computer when the program or programmer has supplied no specific direction at a decision point. *Example:* most microcomputers perform 2's complement fixed-point binary arithmetic as the default action unless the program specifies otherwise.

default disk: in some operating systems, the disk from which the CPU reads or writes whenever the programmer has failed to specify a file. The programmer defaulted by not naming a device and file using a file-specification command.

default value: the predefined value supplied by the computer system when the program does not define what is to be used at a point at which there is more than one possibility.

degauss: to demagnetize anything accidentally or inadvertently magnetized, with a degausser.

degausser: an equipment used to demagnetize. It consists of a current-carrying loop of wire in which a momentary pulse of alternating current is circulated, to rearrange the parallel orientation of magnetic domains to a random disarray.

delete: to remove or eliminate. Most editors and high-level languages for processors and computers have a DELETE command that can remove one character or wipe out an entire line or program.

deletion record: a master-file record that keeps track of the records marked for simultaneous deletion at a later time.

delimit: to establish bounds by inserting markers called delimiters that a computer can recognize and act upon.

delimiter: any symbol used to indicate the limit of something else. *Example:* the use of dollar signs to indicate where one string ends and the adjacent string begins in a long concatenated string: MNOP$HELLO$DOLLY$

DEL key: the delete key, which backs up the screen cursor, electronically erasing every character in its path. Synonymous with RUBOUT, and BACK-SPACE on some keyboards.

delta gun: one of the two configurations for the spatial alignment of the red, green, and blue electron guns in a color CRT or TV tube. The three electron beams form an equilateral triangle. The other type is the in-line configuration, with the three parallel gun axes in a straight line. *See* **in-line gun.**

demand swapping: a memory-management term also called segmented virtual memory. A logic-memory area may still be on the disk when a task tries to access it. Execution of the instruction is postponed until the required memory can be brought into the physical high semiconductor memory.

demodulator: 1: a device that recovers the information previously superimposed on a higher-frequency electromagnetic wave carrier by the process of modulation. 2: the "dem" part of a modem (an abbreviation for a modulator-demodulator), one each required at the ends of a data communications line or link.

density: short for bit packing density, the measure of how much information can be stored on one track or on one side of a floppy disk or another recording medium.

dependent program: a program that is called by an operating system, such as a utility or user program.

DES: data encryption standard, an algorithm originated by the National Bureau of Standards for the encryption of computer output data.

descender: the tail that extends below the typing line of lower-case printed characters: p, q, g, and y all have descenders; d, e, a, etc., do not. Some video terminals and printers that employ dot matrices to form characters print the tail above the line, without true descenders.

descending sort: a numerical sort that orders the items in descending numerical order, from the highest number to the lowest.

description list: a list of data elements and their attributes, in a data-management system.

descriptor: 1: a primitive or elementary word, term, or phrase used to describe a thing, idea, or operation. 2: in information retrieval, a word used to index and categorize data for facilitating recovery later. 3: synonymous with keyword.

development-support library (IBM):   a set of office and computer procedures designed for use in a program development environment to provide constantly up-to-date documentation for programs and test data in both computer and human readable form.

diagnose: to locate and explain hardware or software faults.

diagnostic: 1: a program used by a computer to troubleshoot and fault-isolate its own malfunction or the failure of one of its peripheral units. 2: the tape used to enter a diagnostic program.

diagnostic check, program, or routine: *See* **diagnostic.**

dial-up: the use of a telephone to connect a remote terminal with modem to a distant computer via telephone lines.

dichotomizing search: a search in which an ordered set of items is divided into two parts, one of which is rejected; then the process is repeated on the accepted part until all items with the desired property are found. Synonymous with binary search.

dictionary: 1: a listing of the names of the variables used in a program, procedure, or subroutine with corresponding definitions of their meanings, ranges, units, etc. 2: in a data-management system, a table that specifies the size and format of file variables, assigning each field and record type a data name. Synonymous with data dictionary.

digit: a unique symbol in the set of numbers that make up a number system.

Examples:

Decimal:	0, 1, 2, 3, 4, 5, 6, 7, 8, 9	(10)
Binary:	0, 1	(2)
Octal:	0, 1, 2, 3, 4, 5, 6, 7	(8)
Hexadecimal:	0, 1, 2, 3, 4, 5, 6, 7, 8, 9, A, B, C, D, E, F	(16)

digital: 1: pertaining to calculations and equipment that operate with numerical or discrete units. Mostly, this means working with and processing ones and zeros in a binary system. 2: not analog.

digital incremental plotter: a plotter whose coordinate x and y values change in discrete steps, not continuously as in the case of an analog plotter. *See* **plotter.**

digital readout: the display of data as numbers, as opposed to the analog representation of a quantity as a position, length, color, etc.

digital representation: the representation of a quantity as a number containing digits, as opposed to an analog representation.

digital-to-analog converter: an electronic system of circuits that changes a binary number into a proportional analog voltage. D/A converters are widely used in automatic control and analog displays.

digitizer: any device that converts an analog representation of data into a digital code. The analog data are usually in the form of a large map surface or an expanded scale, accurately dimensioned drawing, and the digitizer is an electro-optical transducer that is moved across the work, producing coded data as it goes.

direct-connect modem: a modem that is designed to be attached to a telephone line by a direct connection, as opposed to an acoustically coupled modem. A modular jack is noramlly used to connect the two. *See* **acoustic coupler;** **modem**.

direct data entry (DDE): the immediate input of data into a computer by some means such as keyboard entry or loading from floppy disk, as opposed to an indirect method such as a card reader, in which the data in the form of punched cards must have been previously prepared off-line.

direct modem: a modem connected directly and electrically to a phone line, not with an acoustic coupler, in which the coupling is by sound waves.

directory: 1: a partition of the magnetic media resources of a computer system assigned to a particular user or function. 2: a file that lists all the files within a directory by their file names or other identifiers.

directory tree: a diagram showing the hierarchy of directories in a computer directory system. See figure on following page.

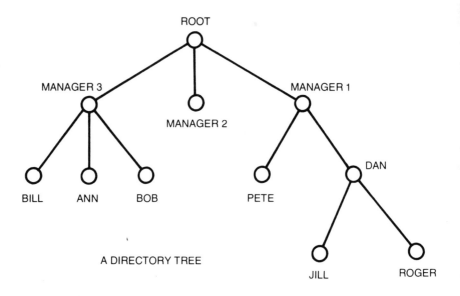

A DIRECTORY TREE

direct-view-storage tube (DVST):   a type of cathode-ray tube that retains images much longer than a raster-scan CRT, even with long persistence phosphors. A unique "flood gun" bombards the screen surface with electrons, greatly increasing the decay period in which the excited phosphor atoms give up photons. DVSTs are used particularly with vector-scan graphic systems.

disc: an alternative and less popular spelling of disk. *See* **disk**.

discette: a rarely seen spelling of diskette. *See* **diskette**.

discrete: not continuous or analog, but digital.

discretionary hyphen: in word processing and typesetting, a hyphen that the operator inserts (at his discretion) wherever he wants a mandatory hyphen. *Example:* in a proper name (Evert-Lloyd) or geographic name (Baden-Baden). If the word falls at the end of a line, the word processor or typesetting computer will hyphenate only at the discretionary hyphen.

disjunctive search: in data-retrieval techniques, a computer search to find all records containing at least one of a set of two or more keys; that is, applying the OR rule, which states that a proposition is true if one or more of its premises are true.

disk: short for magnetic disk. It may refer to a 14-inch-diameter Winchester hard disk used with larger systems, an 8-inch-diameter "floppy," or even a 5.25-inch minidisk or diskette. All are used for bulk storage of computer programs and/or data on a magnetic-material medium. The storage capacity of a hard disk is in the many-megabyte range, whereas a diskette usually can store less than 400 kilobytes. *See* **diskette.**

disk drive: 1: the entire equipment required to record or retrieve digital data from a magnetic disk, diskette, minidisk, floppy disk, etc., including the housing, rotation mechanism, read/write head, and electronics. 2: the rotation mechanism for a disk-drive assembly.

diskette: a small flexible disk, usually 5.25 inches in diameter, used to store computer programs and data on a magnetic surface coating when rotating at high speeds in a disk drive. A single diskette can store almost 400,000 bytes of data (double-sided, dual density) and retrieve any word of it in a few seconds.

disk file: a computer file stored on a magnetic disk.

disk logging: *See* **logging a disk.**

disk operating system (DOS):   a software program, stored on a disk, that allows the user of a microcomputer to perform input/output operations with floppy disks. When power is first applied to a computer, it is virtually helpless, except that it contains a nonvolatile "bootstrap-loader" program that gives it the capability of loading the DOS from the disk into its main semiconductor memory. Once loaded, the DOS programs give the computer the ability to create, open, read from, write to, and manage disk files. Incuded are a number of utility programs that, for example, test memory, initialize new floppy disks, erase files, perform memory dumps, execute the copy of one disk to another, and perform other chores, depending on the particular DOS. A computer is "booted" by loading its DOS from disk to semiconductor main memory. A computer without its DOS is hardly usable.

disk pack: a package resembling a cake holder, containing a set of hard magnetic disks and used to protect the disks from dust and mechanical damage. It is a safe and convenient way to carry several disks from one area to another.

disk reconstruction: a utility for recovering the information from a crashed or damaged disk.

dispatcher: a utility routine in some multiuser or multipurpose operating system software. It maintains a queue of requests for the use of shared I/O resources, arbitrates contentions for their use, and honors requests on a pre-established priority basis.

disperse: to distribute input record items to one or more output records.

dispersed intelligence: a synonym for distributed intelligence.

display: any soft-copy nonrecording visual device for the output of computer information. Some simple 8-bit microcomputers use four 7-segment alpha-numeric LEDs to show the four address-bus digits in hexadecimal code and two 7-segment alphanumeric LEDs that display the data contained at the given address. For larger systems, the usual display is the CRT of a video terminal or monitor.

display attribute: a synonym for a video attribute, also known as a visual attribute: blink, inverse video, underline (underscore), half intensity, etc.

display console: a synonym for a video terminal.

display control: an equipment that interfaces a number of terminals (display consoles) to a central processing unit.

display menu: synonymous with menu; the options listed on a CRT screen for use by a computer operator, who types in or uses a light pen to input a selected response.

display tube: a cathode-ray tube (CRT).

distributed processing: 1: decentralization of computer power within a given company, system, building, organization, or vehicle. Until the development of minicomputers and microcomputers, the practice was to concentrate everything in one large central computer that was supposed to be all things to all users. Now the trend is reversed. In a multiprocessor system, many processors communicate with each other under the direction of one processor at a time acting as controller. Distributed processing is also a more general term that may refer to a multiprocessor or merely to the existence of two or more independent, isolated, autonomous computer systems. 2: loosely, multiprocessing.

distribution disk: the floppy disk you get when you buy a software package. Good practice says you should immediately make a back-up working copy and then store the distribution disk in a safe place, but not in the same area with your computer.

document: 1: to record on paper or some other medium all the comments, flowcharts, diagrams, pseudocodes, and codes necessary for complete understanding of software programs, not only by the programmer but also by other programmers and users. Top-level documentation should also be understandable to nonprogrammers, such as managers and hardware people. 2: a series of related pages. 3: a general term for any printed or typed text.

document assembly: the integration of two or more documents into a single document (some word processors).

domain: 1: a field of action, thought, or influence. 2: a realm or range of personal knowledge, responsibility, etc. 3: the set of values assigned to the independent variable or variables of a function.

domain (magnetic):   a homogeneous region in a magnetic material in which the tiny magnetic poles of the chemical elements that compose the material are all aligned in the same direction.

DOS: disk operating system. A computer's operating system software stored on a disk. When power is first applied to a computer that has had power removed, its only program is a small hardware semiconductor "bootstrap loader" that gives it the ability to operate and read from its disk-drive mechanism in response to keyboard command inputs. The operator must "boot up the system" by following keyboard procedures that cause the operating system software to be read from the disk and stored in the main semiconductor memory. The computer then has all its specified capabilities.

dot commands: in MicroPro's WordStar word-processing software, a feature that lets you customize printouts. A dot-command line begins with a dot that tells the computer that the line that follows is not part of the text to be printed but instead is a command to be executed. Dot commands specify margin widths, line spacing, the number of characters per inch, etc. Two dots indicate that the line is a comment.

dot matrix: a technique used by some printers to form characters, such as alphabetics, numerals, and punctuation symbols. The dots necessary to form the character are selected from a rectangular array of dots, usually 5×7 or 6×8.

dot-matrix character: a character printed by selecting the appropriate dots in a rectangular array (matrix) to form the desired pattern. The following figure shows dot-matrix characters. *See* **fully formed character; matrix.**

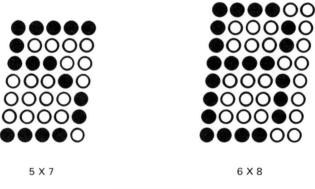

5 X 7   6 X 8

DOT MATRICES

dot-matrix printer: a mechanism that prints dot-matrix characters. Several types of print mechanisms are used.

double buffering: a technique used in some raster-scan graphics processors to achieve higher-speed operation. A duplicate set of memory planes is written while the first is read and its contents are transferred to the screen. Without double buffering, writing can take place only during the flyback period of the electron beam.

double density: a term applied to magnetic-storage media such as disks and tapes that can store twice as many bits per inch as a standard (single-density) unit. Synonymous with dual density.

double precision: a term describing a fixed-point arithmetic operation executed with two-word operands for greater precision. When only single-word operations are used, the arithmetic is called single precision.

double-precision arithmetic: *See* **double precision**.

double-sided: pertaining to some floppy disks that have recording surfaces and tracks on both sides; generally they are dual density as well, and store close to four times the data that a single-sided, single-density disk can.

double-striking: a feature of some word processors and other automatic printers that can back up and overprint characters by striking them twice, making a bolder print for emphasis.

down: describing a computer that is not operating due to a malfunction, power outage, periodic maintenance, etc. The opposite is "up and running."

DOWN key: in some word processors, a keyboard key used to print characters above the line for superscripts and below the line for subscripts, simulating the turning of the platen knob on a typewriter.

downtime: the period during which a computer is unavailable or not operating due to a malfunction or periodic maintenance.

DRAM: an acronym for dynamic random-access memory; it is popular with the computer graphics manufacturers who will use prodigious amounts of these chips in the future. *See* **dynamic RAM**.

drive: short for disk or tape drive.

drive cover: in a disk drive, the door that closes the opening into which the disk is inserted. The drive cover must be closed whenever the disk is rotating.

drum: short for magnetic drum, an obsolescent bulk memory-storage device. *See* **magnetic drum.**

drum printer: a high-speed printer mechanism that uses a cylindrical drum embossed with fully formed type characters. As the drum rotates at high speed, a computer-driven hammer strikes the paper from behind at the exact instant the desired character on the drum passes the position at which the letter is to be printed. There is a complete set of characters for each character position in the line. Each character set is embossed in a circumferential track in a plane perpendicular to the axis of rotation of the drum, one parallel track for each character in the line. The hammer traverses axially down the cylinder as it rotates, printing at high rates.

DTE: data-transmitting equipment, one of two classes of RS-232C bus standard equipments. The other is DCE (data communications equipment).

dumb: describing an equipment lacking a computer with its associated "intelligence." The opposite is a smart device, usually containing a microprocessor or microcomputer. The most common reference is to a dumb terminal.

dumb dot-matrix printer: a printer capable of printing just a single fixed-character set, usually a low resolution 5 × 7, rather than many different fonts, changed under software control. *See* **smart dot-matrix printer.**

dumb terminal: a computer video terminal with no microprocessor to give it "intelligence" and make it a "smart" terminal.

dummy: 1: an artificial argument, address, statement, instruction, etc., inserted in a program to fulfill a prescribed condition, allowing the computer to run without affecting it in any other way. 2: having the appearance and form of a specified thing but not the capacity to function as such. *Example:* a dummy plug.

duplex: in communications, pertaining to a simultaneous independent transmission in both directions. Synonymous with full duplex. A half-duplex system can transmit in both directions but not simultaneously.

duplex channel: a data communications channel that supports simultaneous transmissions in both directions. Short for full duplex. *See* **half duplex**; **simplex**.

duplex computer: a computer-system configuration employing two central processors: one in operation at all times; the other on standby, ready to come on line if and when the operating unit goes down, either due to equipment failure or periodic maintenance.

duplication check: in data processing, a test operation in which the same problem (usually a calculation) is solved by each of two independent methods, and the results are then compared.

durability: the extent to which a program can be used for similar but not identical applications, with modifications if necessary.

duty cycle: the percentage of the total elapsed time a device is running or operating; a fan motor that is on 15 minutes of every hour and off for the remaining 45 minutes has a 25% duty cycle.

Dvorak keyboard: a computer keyboard layout in which the most frequently used letters fall under the fingers in the "home row" where the hand rests, as opposed to the conventional QWERTY keyboard of typewriters and terminals with a, s, d, f and j, k, l, ; in home row.

dyadic operator: a mathematical or logical operator indicated by juxtaposition of two variables, without an operator symbol between them. *Examples:* in digital logic, the AND relation AB; in vectors, AB, indicating the dot product, $A \cdot B$.

dynamic: pertaining to or characterized by action; not static.

dynamic font change: a feature of some high-resolution dot-matrix printers that can change typeface in the middle of a word, line, or page under program control. Each font is determined by read-only memory patterns that select the particular dots needed to implement a given character.

dynamic memory: *See* **dynamic storage**.

dynamic RAM: a dynamic random-access read/write memory. *See* **dynamic storage**.

dynamic segment relocation: a memory-management technique in which user software addresses are independent of physical memory locations, which are assigned at run time by the memory-management unit (MMU). The user does not have to assign physical (absolute) addresses. In fact, he could not if he wanted to. That's the whole idea.

dynamic storage: a memory device, usually capacitive, that must be constantly recharged or "refreshed" at frequent intervals (a few milliseconds) to avoid loss of data; a very volatile memory. Dynamic memories are usually smaller for the same amount of storage than static memories.

dynamic store: (British): synonymous with dynamic memory.

dynaturtle: in LOGO language, a dynamic turtle. A static turtle has a fixed *x–y* position and heading, whereas a dynaturtle has a constant velocity or acceleration. *See* **turtle**.

ECC: *See* **error-correction code**.

echo: to send or repeat back transmitted data over a communications link, usually for error detection but sometimes as the result of a malfunction. If a computer has not crashed, a Control C typed at the keyboard should be echoed on the CRT.

echo check: a method of testing the accuracy of transmitted data in which the data as received at the other end of the line are returned to the sender for bit-by-bit comparison with the original data.

edge connector: an electrical male (pins) or female (socket) on the edge of a printed-circuit or wire-wrap board for connecting it into a mother board or external cable harness. Also called a card-edge connector.

edit: to remove, insert, relocate, or correct parts of a computer program or text.

editor: a software or firmware tool, a program or part of a program purchased for a specific computer as an aid in modifying, editing, rewriting, changing, or debugging a program being developed. It greatly eases the chore of inserting or deleting instructions. Some automatically renumber the instructions and produce a new program listing with revised numbers. It may be a line editor, a screen editor, or a text editor.

edit routine: synonymous with editor.

EDP: electronic data processing, an obsolescent term. It has been all electronic for years.

EFT: *See* **electronic funds transfer**.

eight-level code: describing the prevalent teletype transmission and punch tape code to distinguish from the five-level Baudot code used in the older machines.

eighty-column card: a synonym for the Hollerith punch card, familiarly known as an IBM card, an obsolescent input/output storage method involving cardboard cards punched with 80 punched columns of coded data.

electrographic printer: a synonym for an electrostatic printer.

electronic cut-and-paste: the ability of word processors and text and screen editors to move blocks of text characters—words, sentences, whole paragraphs, etc.—from one part of a text file being edited to another place in the text. The analogy to the old editing use of scissors and glue on paper draft copies is obvious.

electronic funds transfer (EFT): the automatic transfer of the coded equivalent of funds from one institution to another, via computers. EFT is largely responsible for increased markets for data-encryption hardware and software in an attempt to reduce computer crimes.

electronic mail: the automatic transfer of printed correspondence (letters, memos, invoices, statements, etc.) from computer to computer, interoffice and intraoffice. The received message may be displayed on a CRT or output to a printer for hard copy.

electronic publishing: 1: in its general sense, radio and television; data-retrieval services that transmit information into homes and offices as modulations of the TV carrier frequency. 2: the production, distribution, and sale of high-volume computer software, usually for entertainment or educational purposes.

electrosensitive printer: a dot-matrix printing technology that prints characters by burning dots into a special paper. A print head employs high-static voltages to vaporize dots of a light-colored, metallized paper coating, exposing a dark background that then shows through.

electrostatic storage: a memory technology in which binary data are represented by the presence or absence of an electrostatic charge in prescribed areas of a nonconducting surface, such as a CRT screen.

element: 1: a single data item, such as one value in an array or string. 2: a obsolete term for a hardware gate.

elite: a common type character design and font, more delicate than pica, that prints at 12 pitch (12 characters per inch).

em: 1: the letter m. 2: in printing and typesetting, the typeset dimension of an em quad, used as a unit of measure for the wider letters m and w.

em dash: in typesetting, a dash equal in width to an em quad, and wider than an en dash. *See* **em; en.**

empirical: pertaining to data, a statement, or a relationship between variables, based on experimental or observed results, and not predicted or supported by any theory.

em space: a typeset space equal in width to an em quad, and wider than an en space. *See* **em; en.**

en: 1: the letter n. 2: in typesetting, the typeset dimension of an en quad used as a unit of measure. *See* **em; measure; quad.**

encipher: to encode for purposes of security and secrecy.

encode: 1: to put into code; synonymous with code. 2: to convert from one system of communication to another. 3: to put into a particular code format.

encoder: any device that encodes.

encrypt: 1: synonymous with encipher. 2: to encode for security and secrecy. Data encryption seems to be a more popular term than enciphering today.

encryption: the result of encrypting or encoding.

en dash: a narrow dash, equal in width to an en quad but narrower than an em dash. *See* **em; en.**

end-of-file character (EOF): a control character recorded at the end of a file stored on magnetic media to indicate just that.

end-of-file indicator: a synonym for end-of-file mark.

end-of-file mark (EOF): any hardware or software indication that the end of a file has been reached and that no more data can be written to it.

end-of-medium character (EM): a teletypewriter control character transmitted to indicate that the end of a recording medium has been reached.

end-of-message character (EOM): in data communications, a control character sent to denote the end of the message just transmitted.

end-of-tape mark (EOT): usually, a reflective spot on the back (noncoated) side of a magnetic tape, a few feet from the physical end. It is sensed by photoelectric devices to indicate to drive motor-control circuits the approach of the end of the tape.

end-of-transmission character (EOT): in data transmission, a character sent to denote the end of that transmission.

enqueue: to put data items into a program queue. *See* **queue**.

en space: a narrow space, equal in width to an en quad, as opposed to the wider em space. It's wider than a thin space, however. *See* **em**; **en**.

entry: 1: the first instruction in the subroutine; therefore, the entry point of the routine. 2: the first instruction in a program.

entry block: a region of memory in which the first location is an entry.

entry conditions: the initial data and control conditions that must be satisfied before a given subroutine can be executed successfully.

entry point: any place a subroutine or procedure may be entered, to which control may be passed. In structured programming, each proper procedure can have only one entry point and only one exit.

entry time: the instant that control is transferred to an application program from a supervisory routine.

environment: 1: the physical conditions (temperature, humidity, vibration, air purity, etc.) in which a computer must operate. 2: the mode of operation of a computer system. *Examples:* the multitasking environment, the multiuser environment.

EOF: the end-of-file character or mark. *See* **end-of-file character.**

EOLN function: in PASCAL, a Boolean function (true or false) that is true when the end of a line is detected and false otherwise.

EOT: 1: the end-of-tape mark. *See* **end-of-tape mark.** 2: the end-of-transmission character, a data-transmission control character.

EPROM: erasable programmable read-only memory, a PROM that can be programmed electrically, like other PROMs, but this one can be erased using an ultraviolet light and then reprogrammed. If erased properly with the proper UV light intensity and time of exposure, EPROMs can be erased and reprogrammed 100 or more times. The EPROM is the program memory most frequently used by the small system, the experimenter, hobbyist, phototyper, etc., and anyone else who must make frequent changes in the program. One can do it oneself with the proper equipment—a PROM programmer, often called a PROM burner.

erase: 1: to remove data from a magnetic medium, either accidentally or by intention. Magnetic tapes and disks are susceptible to strong magnetic fields. Data are intentionally erased by creating a strong, steady magnetic field that will leave all magnetic domains saturated in the same polarity and direction (e.g., N-S, representing a digital 1). 2: to remove data intentionally, usually, by exposing an EPROM or EROM to ultraviolet light for 18 minutes or so, which will erase all data on the entire chip.

erase character: a character inserted in a block of recorded or stored data to mark it for erasure at a later time. Synonymous with ignored character.

erase head: a permanent magnet "head" in some tape transports, located just before the tape passes the read/write head. The steady magnetic field produced by the head causes total erasure of all data previously recorded on the tape. *See* **erase**.

ergonomics: a synonym for biotechnology and used in the computer world by the marketers of office furniture: desks, chairs, workstations, and displays, suggesting or implying that they were designed with human factors in mind.

EROM: erasable read-only memory. An EPROM.

error character: a character inserted in recorded data to mark an error so that it can be ignored until it is removed at a later time, probably with other errors. Also known as an ignore character.

error-checking code: a general term for an error-correction or error-detection code.

error-correction code (ECC):   a code capable of detecting an error in a digital word or character, identifying the wrong bit or bits and replacing them with the right ones. *Examples:* the Hamming codes and block parity.

error-correction routine: a program written to detect and correct errors in a transmitted data message, using an error-correction code.

error-detection code: a code that can detect one or more errors in a binary word or character but cannot identify the erroneous bit(s) and replace it with the correct ones. The most commonly used error-detection code is the simple parity check. Also known as a self-checking code.

error-detection routine: a program written to detect errors in a transmitted message but not to correct them.

error diagnostic: a compiler subprogram or routine that checks the source language statements during a compilation and prints error messages identifying what errors were made and where.

error handler: a software routine or procedure that defines the action to be taken when a predefined error occurs. The CPU will trap to the location of the starting instruction of the error handler when the error happens.

error list: synonymous with error listing.

error listing: 1: a list of programming errors produced by an assembler at the end of its program run. 2: a list of error messages for a high-level language.

error message: a coded number output by a high-level language compiler or interpreter to annunciate a program error. The code may appear at the time the error is committed during the programming, or it may not be output until the program runs. Error messages are displayed on printers and video terminals and are listed in the user's manual for the programming language. *Example:* when programming in BASIC, error message 1, Improper Syntax, appeared, indicating that the last instruction typed and entered had a syntax error and was rejected by the interpreter. Some ROM BASIC interpreters will not have alphabetic error messages; they will only have decimal error codes.

error range: the range of values of a variable that it cannot or should not have; any value within this range will be regarded as an error.

error rate: the frequency at which errors occur. Technically, the ratio of the total number of errors in a transmission to the total number of correct characters transmitted, expressed, for example, as 1×10^{-9}. Error rate is used most often in the transmission and recording of digital data to specify required accuracy.

error recovery routine: *See* **recovery routine**.

error routine: a subroutine or procedure that specifies how a given run-time error in a computer program is to be handled when it arises. The CPU will trap to the starting location of the error program in memory. Synonymous with recovery routine and error handler.

error tape: in magnetic recording, a tape on which data known to contain errors are written for later analysis.

error trapping: a hardware and software technique in which a detected error causes the program to "trap" (go and execute) to some predetermined error recovery routine. It could be a simple halt.

ESC: the escape character, a nonprinting control character for video terminals and printers.

escape: to recover from an undesirable or uncontrolled computer program condition. Most computer terminal keyboards have an escape key that returns control to the monitor or supervisor routine when it is necessary to recover from a bad situation during a program run.

escape character (ESC):   a nonprinting control character used with one or more succeeding characters to form an "escape sequence," a code-extending technique used in the communication of a keyboard terminal with a computer. *Example:* the cursor for the Lear-Siegler ADM3A Video Terminal may be positioned with an escape sequence as follows: escape key, = key, Row ASCII, Column ASCII. ESC,=6,N will position the cursor in row 23, column 47.

escape code: a printer or video terminal control code, called an escape sequence, consisting of the ASCII ESC key code (27 decimal), followed by an alphanumeric or symbolic character. The ESC identifies the sequence as a control code, and the second byte is a modifier that specifies the function. In general, printer escape sequences are not standard, and every computer and printer manufacturer has his own. Be wary.

escape key: one of the usual set of keys on the keyboard of a terminal, usually identified with ESC or ↑ (up arrow) on the key face. When struck, it generates the escape character.

ESDI: enhanced small-disk interface, one of many attempts among disk-drive manufacturers to achieve some kind of standard.

EtherNET: a local data communications network developed by Xerox, Digital Equipment Corporation, and Intel Corporation with the goal of establishing it as an industry standard for distributed-processing and office-automation applications. These systems require devices to be linked over relatively short distances (a few hundred feet) throughout an office building or industrial complex.

event: 1: in business programming, any action that necessitates a change to the existing files: a sale, a purchase, a received payment, etc. 2: one access to a file to either read or write (a file event).

event-driven: pertaining to the passing of control from one part of a program to another when a predetermined event occurs. *Examples:* an interrupt from an I/O device, a test input change, a front-panel switch closure.

exchangeable disk store (EDS): (British): a generic term for a disk drive that employs removable plastic disks (floppies), as opposed to a hard-disk drive, which uses one nonremovable disk for data storage.

exchange buffering: a memory-management technique in which user buffer-memory areas are exchanged as necessary with the larger system buffer-memory areas, avoiding the movement of data within main memory.

execute: 1: to put into action. 2: to perform a given instruction after it has been fetched from memory. 3: to run a program or subroutine.

executive program: 1: the part of a computer program that will end up in machine code and will be executed, as opposed to assembler directives, which are merely guidance to the assembling computer and will not appear in the object-code listing. An executable program. 2: a management or supervisory main program that handles priority scheduling, timing, interrupt servicing, I/O control, from which all main subroutines and procedures are called.

executive routine: synonymous with executive program or supervisory routine.

exhaustivity: in information retrieval, the number of keywords assigned to a record in a file.

exit: the instant in time or a point in the procedure or subroutine at which control returns to the program from which it was called.

exit point: the instruction in a program listing that returns control back to the calling program.

expander board: synonymous with expansion card, although a physically larger unit is implied.

expansion card: a card added to a system for mounting additional integrated circuits or discrete components to expand the system capability.

exponent: the number or pair of numbers representing the power to which the base number is to be raised. *See* **exponentiation**. An exponent is normally printed as a superscript in mathematical literature, but computer keyboards and printers usually cannot do this, so exponents are indicated by double asterisks, as in $2**3 = 8$, or $2\uparrow3 = 8$, where 3 is the exponent or power to which 2 is raised to get the result, 8.

exponentiation: the process of raising a number to a power. On computer keyboards or printouts, exponentiation is denoted in some systems by the double asterisks ** and in others by an up arrow, ↑, because the typical keyboard has no way to print superscripts. *See* **exponent**.

exposed recording surface: the parts of a floppy disk that show through the various holes and access apertures and are not protected by the cardboard or plastic jacket. Avoid fingerprinting, dirtying, or damaging these surfaces; otherwise, a disaster is on its way.

expression: any valid combination of mathematical or logic variables, constants, and operation symbols. $A = B \cdot C$ is a valid logic expression, and ABS $(\sin (X + Y)) + C$ is a valid mathematical expression in BASIC.

extended binary-coded-decimal interchange code (EBCDIC): a serial character code for transmission of digital information. Sometimes called expanded binary-coded-decimal interchange code. It is being superseded by ASCII.

extender: short for a card or board extender—a hardware troubleshooting tool that allows the board to operate outside the confinement of its case or chassis so test leads and clips can be applied or so it may operate outside of the temperature environment of the chassis. The module to be extended is unplugged from its socket; the extended board is plugged in its place, and then the module is plugged into the top of the extender board for operating.

external label: the paper label placed on the outside of a canned reel of magnetic tape, as opposed to the label written on the tape by the read/write head.

extract: to remove a selected part from a set or group.

facsimile (FAX): a process, technique, and equipment for transmitting pictures, usually of documents, such as weather maps, from one point to a distant station, perhaps thousands of miles away. The transmitting equipment scans the document and converts it into coded signals that can be transmitted over ordinary telephone lines. The signals are recovered at the receiving end, decoded, and constructed into a recorded copy of the original.

fade: a decreasing intensity in a fluctuating received transmission signal.

failsafe: pertaining to a system or an equipment designed to recover from a malfunction or hardware/software failure without dangerous anomalies from normal operation, although some degraded performance is acceptable.

failsoft programming: a programming practice of writing routines so that failures and errors will usually result in degraded operation rather than outright failure.

failure logging: the automatic recording of hardware or software defects for later analysis and correction.

failure rate: a quantitative estimate of the reliability of a part or equipment, stated as the number of failures in a given number of hours. Failure rate is calculated by recording the total number of failures in the set and dividing it by the sum of the operating hours for all the members of the group.

fanfold paper: a continuous-feed form paper for a printer, usually high speed. As it runs out of the printer and into a receiving tray or basket, it piles itself into pages, folding alternately at perforations at the top and then at the bottom of each page—well, usually.

fast key: a control key that, when held down simultaneously with a repeating key, increases the repetition rate (some keyboards).

fatal error: an error from which there is no recovery. It generally means lost work and lost time and requires a new start.

father: pertaining to a file or disk that has been copied; the copies are sons. If any one of the sons is copied, the son becomes a father and the father becomes a grandfather. Such is life. Since this may happen over a period of time, and each one may be modified, it is quite likely that the copies are no longer identical and each may bear only a family resemblance to another.

fault: an equipment or software failure. *Examples:* a transistor breakdown, shorted diode, broken connector pin.

fault time: (British): a synonym for downtime.

fault-tolerant: describing an equipment or software that suffers no significant degradation in operation or performance when one or more faults occur.

feed reel: the reel from which tape is wound during a reel-to-reel transfer. The other reel is the take-up reel.

FIB: a popular abbreviation for focused ion beam, an emerging technology for fabricating the next generation semiconductor RAMS and other SLSI (super-large-scale integration) and ULSI (ultra-large-scale integration) chips. *See* **focused ion beam**.

Fibonacci number: an integer in a Fibonacci series. *See* **Fibonacci series**.

Fibonacci search: a dichotomizing search such that in each step of the search the orginal set or remaining subset is subdivided in accordance with successively smaller numbers in the Fibonacci series. If the number of items in the set is not equal to a Fibonacci number, the number of items in the set is assumed to equal the next higher Fibonacci number.

Fibonacci series: a series of integers in which each integer is equal to the sum of the two preceding integers in the series. The series is formulated mathematically as $x_i = x_{i-1} + x_{i-2}$, where $x_0 = 0$, $x_1 = 1$; that is $0, 1, 2, 3, 5, 8, 13, 21. \ldots$

field: an area allocated for a specific function or purpose in a code format. *Examples:* the first four bits in an instruction word, reserved for the operation code (the opcode field); the first column of an assembly-language program listing, assigned to labels (the label field of the program listing).

field length: in a computer word format, the number of bits assigned to the field.

file: 1: a large quantity of related data, usually stored in a bulk memory peripheral unit and read into the main CPU memory when required. 2: a collection of related records treated as a unit.

file activity ratio: the number of records (or other file elements) for which a transaction has occurred during a specified number of program runs, divided by the total number of records in the file.

file attribute: a distinctive file feature that can be set or changed by the user via system calls or operating system commands. *Example:* a file may be assigned a read-only attribute by its owner/manager, permitting other users to access the file for the purpose of reading the information only. Altering the file or appending more data would be denied.

file character count: the number of characters from the start of the file to the cursor, in word processing. If you want an exact count, subtract 1.

file characteristic: a distinctive file feature that cannot be changed by the user. *Example:* my operating system will not accept file names greater than eight ASCII characters, and even some of these characters, such as - and space, are excluded.

file conversion: the conversion of a data file from one format to another or from one medium to another.

file directory: a file that lists the files on a disk by their file names or other identifiers. My disks can have up to 128 directory files per disk; each directory shows the number of bytes used in each file as well. Sometimes in big systems you need a directory of directories.

file event: one access to a file, either a read transaction or a write transaction. Shortened to event, sometimes.

file extent: a specified file area of contiguous tracks on a secondary storage medium. Synonymous with file section.

file index menu: a synonym for a directory, a list of current files on a disk or tape.

file label: the first record or block in a file, containing file identification data. Synonymous with header block or record. A file label may include a file number, reel or disk identification number, data written, and a description of the file contents.

file layout: a written definition of the organization and contents of a file.

file line count: the number of lines from the start of a file to the cursor, in word processing. If you need an exact count, subtract 1.

file maintenance: the process of keeping a file up-to-date by modifying and appending where necessary.

file manager: an operating system subroutine that controls file access, implements file security, and catalogues files.

file name: the string of alphanumeric characters and symbols assigned to identify a file. The operating system for each computer will have its own specific rules for establishing a file name. Pick a name with a mnemonic quality, if possible, or one that is amenable to the various alphabet or numeric sort routines. ALPHA1.BAK and SCREEN.COM are examples of file names with file extensions. *See* **file-name extension.**

file-name extension: the characters added to a file name, usually following a period, that identify the type of data in the file. The following file extensions are common in most systems: .BAK, a backup file; .BAS, a BASIC file; .FOR, a FORTRAN file; and .COM, a command file.

file print: (British): a printout of the contents of a file, usually for file checking or debugging.

file processing: the operations involved in the use of files: creating, comparing, copying, collating, merging, sorting, validating, etc. Files are processed by operating system utilities, word processors, and data-base manager programs.

file protection: any hardware or software methods used to prevent the accidental overwriting and potential loss of file data. Some common precautions are the gummed stickers applied (or sometimes removed) over the write-protect notch to prevent inadvertent writing to a floppy disk or the write-permit or write-inhibit rings inserted into magnetic-tape reels for the same purpose. There are many software precautions that may be taken to protect files from careless loss of data.

file purging: the intentional erasing of a file, usually at a predetermined date established when the file was created, or perhaps when its contents are no longer needed.

file reconstitution: the restoration and updating of a file that has been partially destroyed, usually as a result of a disk-head crash or some other disaster.

file recovery: the updating of a file that has not been properly maintained for some reason, perhaps an extended system downtime.

file reel: synonymous with supply reel, the reel in reel-to-reel tape units that is the source of the tape going to the other reel, the take-up reel.

file section: a synonym for file extent.

file security: the relative safety of a file from intentional or inadvertent access or alteration by unauthorized users. The increasing need for file security (for example, in electronic funds transfer and electronic mail) is spawning a growing market for encryption hardware and software. *See* **file protection**.

file specification: the unique identification of a particular file. A complete file specification defines the file name, file type, physical location, and, perhaps most important, the file version number.

file store: (British): the files of an operating system, stored on disk or some other secondary storage medium.

file-type extender or extension: a synonym for a file-name extension.

file version number: the modifier added to a file name or other identifier that uniquely defines the version of a particular file. Most files are very dynamic things, subject to constant change. The existence of several unidentified versions of a file with the same file could create a real mess. The file version number may be simply a date and time code.

filing disk: in word processing, a floppy disk that is used to store text and typed material, as opposed to a program disk that stores the operative programs.

fill: to insert fill characters into a fixed-length record to make the number of characters equal to the specified record length, when the data itself is less than this value. *See* **fill character**.

fill character: a printing character used to fill out a fixed-length record by adding it after the data characters, which are too few to have the required record length. The fill character is usually some letter, like a small x in a record of capital letters, or any other symbol that the software can recognize as a nondata character.

FIND: a word-processing command that locates a specified word, phrase, or string when executed. The command word FIND is generally followed by delimiters enclosing the phrase or string to be found. The backslash character, \, is often used. Synonymous with search for.

firmware: microcomputer programs or data that have been implemented in a ROM, PROM, EROM, EEROM, EE-ROM, EAROM, EPROM, etc., as opposed to software programs stored on paper or magnetic media that must be entered into a RAM to be used. Firmware memories are nonvolatile and will be right there even if the power is turned off or lost.

five level: pertaining to the older teletype and punched tape that used the 5-bit Baudot code, plus start and stop bits, to form a character. You do not see much of this code any more.

fixed-point arithmetic: one of the two major types of computer arithmetic processes, the other being floating point. Fixed-point arithmetic assumes that each operand is an integer with its binary point to the right of the LSB. It is the work of the programmer to keep track of the binary-point position following an arithmetic operation, just as in using a slide rule. *See* **floating-point arithmetic.**

fixed-point calculations: *See* **fixed-point arithmetic.**

fixed-program computer: a computer with a constant, nonchanging program implementing a special-purpose computer for one given application, as opposed to a general-purpose computer with variable programs. Synonymous with dedicated computer.

flag character: markers that appear on a word processing screen to convey special information. *Example:* in MicroPro's WordStar, a + at the end of a line indicates that the line that follows it is a continuation of it, not a separate line. (This is a common problem when processing documents that are wider than the screen's 80 characters.)

flicker: the distortion that occurs in a TV or graphics display monitor when alternating fields of the display are updated too infrequently. For flicker-free operation, the picture must be refreshed at least 30 times per second.

flippy: (British): a floppy disk.

floating point: *See* **floating-point arithmetic.**

floating-point arithmetic: the arithmetic in which a number is expressed as coefficient (mantissa) multiplied by a power of the base of the number system. In most minicomputers, the base is 16. The radix point is assumed to be left of the most significant digit, making the mantissa a fraction. The power may be positive or negative.

floating-point coefficient: *See* **floating-point arithmetic.**

floating-point compaction: a rarely used reference to the floating-point number system, which does compact data on paper. But hardly in the computer.

floppy: short for floppy disk or floppy-disk drive.

floppy disk: a bulk-storage random-access memory technology. A flexible, circular disk coated with a magnetic material on which data can be stored. Floppy disks may be 5¼ or 8 inches in diameter, with recording surfaces on one side or both. Data may be recorded in single or dual density with soft or hard sectoring.

floppy-disk controller chip: a single LSI integrated circuit that replaces all the electronics formerly required to implement a floppy-disk controller, the hardware interface between a computer and a floppy-disk drive. A Nippon Electric Corporation (NEC) design executes 15 complex commands, including many subroutines usually found in disk-handler software. It interfaces with all popular microprocessors. It can execute complex commands such as multiple-sector read/write and multiple-drive seeks, and it controls up to four double-sided disk drives.

floppy-disk drive: the mechanism that rotates a floppy disk at high speeds to provide quick random access to files and records. A floppy-disk drive includes the electronics that control the starting and stopping of the drive motor and the reading and writing of data from and to the disk. Floppy-disk units are microcomputer compatible but expensive for the average hobby budget. For the small business, or, in fact, any other serious application for computers, they represent the lowest cost approach for storage of large quantities of computer data and programs with reasonably short access times.

floppy-disk loader: an interfacing device, hardware and/or software, that enables the CPU to read or write to a floppy disk.

flowchart: a graphic representation of the sequential steps and organization of a computer program to solve a problem. The construction of a flowchart is one of the first steps in writing a program. It acts as a road map in laying out the structure of the program before it is converted into instruction codes or statements. The programmer first lays out a broad-brush general flowchart, replacing it with more detailed flowcharts on the second and successive rounds. Plastic templates with standard symbols are available to facilitate construction.

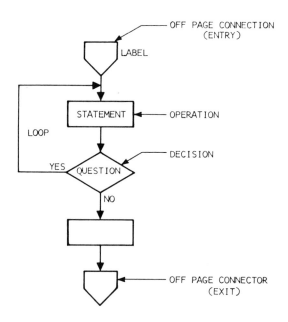

flow lines: the interconnecting lines in a flowchart.

flow-process diagram: a systems flowchart.

flush left: describing a line position in which the first character is at the left-hand page margin.

flush right: describing a line position in which the last character is lined up with the right-hand page margin, in a justified text.

flying-disk drive: a floppy-disk technology.

flying-spot scanner: in optical character recognition, a device that moves a spot of light to scan a sample space and senses the intensity of the reflected light with a photoelectric transducer.

focused ion beam (FIB):   an emerging semiconductor fabrication technology expected to replace photolithography because it can make finer lines and areas, increasing component densities. A 1-megabit RAM is predicted for the mid-1980s, with four megabits by 1990.

folio: 1: a leaf or page in a document. 2: a page number. 3: to put a page number on each leaf or page in a book.

font: 1: the size, shape, and design of a set of print characters. 2: the interchangeable print head that contains a character set, all of one size and style. *Examples:* IBM Selectric Courier 12, Manifold, and Orator spherical ball fonts.

font-editor utility: a software program that facilitates the design of user-defined characters for computer displays having dot-addressable character cells.

footer: the text placed at the bottom of a page of text; as a minimum, the footer consists of a page number, perhaps with a letter prefix.

footprint: the horizontal area (board, desk, or floor space) that an equipment requires. A marketing term.

forbidden: synonymous with illegal; use with instruction codes, file-name characters, etc.

force justify: in automatic typesetting, a command that, when appended to the end of a line of input text, will cause it to fill out to the right margin.

foreground-background interface: a time-share service term describing the rules the user must observe for proper operation of the "foreground" programs on the time-share computer in the "background" (that is, in a batch mode at some later time).

foreground processing: the execution of predesignated high-priority computer programs that preempt the use of the facilities by background users or programs that simply must wait. *See* **background processing.**

foreground program: a time-share service term describing the source program that is entered by a driver program into the time-share computer for batch processing in the "background" at a later time, usually at a lower price.

format: 1: the predetermined mandatory order, organization, or positions of symbols in a computer instruction, data or I/O word, data-transmission message, program statement, or listing, etc.; the order is mandatory so that the computer can understand and interpret the information. 2: to adapt the order and organization of code symbols in a coded word for proper input to or output from a computer or its peripheral device.

format status line: a line at the top or bottom of a word-processor screen that displays information on operating mode, page number, commands, etc.

formatter: a software utility that forms a part of a word-processing package; the total software consists of a screen or text editor and a formatter. The formatter controls how the finished text will appear on paper, setting margins, paragraphing, titles, headers, footers, line spacing, justifying, beautifying, etc., in accordance with operator commands.

form feed: a one-page advance on a printer, actuated by a nonprinting form-feed character.

form-feed character: a nonprinting control character transmitted by the computer to a printer to advance the paper form or roll.

form flash: (British): a synonym for a form overlay.

form overlay: the display of a stored form on a video terminal to simulate the use of a printed form.

form stop: a mechanical device that stops a printer when the paper runs out.

FORTRAN (Formula Translation Language): a high-level, problem-oriented programming language used principally by engineers and scientists. It is similar to BASIC but much more powerful and more demanding in its use. Although there are ANSI-standard FORTRANs, there are many variations of the language: FORTRAN II, FORTRAN IV, FORTRAN-80, etc. FORTRAN is an abbreviation for formula translator and is almost always compiled rather than interpreted.

four-wire channel: a data-transmission circuit that has a two-wire transmitting path and a two-wire receiving path between sender and receiver, allowing simultaneous transmitting and receiving (full-duplex operation).

frame: 1: a subdivision of a message in digital communications. In serial transmission, the data character is said to be "framed" by the start and stop bits. The exact definition of what constitutes a frame is system-dependent. 2: one image in a display.

frame buffer: in a bit-mapped computer graphics system, a memory plane that stores a full frame of picture data. The image must be refreshed, one raster line at a time, at least 30 times per second to avoid flicker.

frame rate: in video technology, the number of complete pictures transmitted per second.

frequency: the number of repetitions of a periodic process in a unit of time. The number of complete alterations per second of an alternating voltage or current.

front end: the terminal or input device in a computer system.

front matter: the information at the front end of a book or document: Library of Congress identification numbers, copyright data, title, table of contents, list of illustrations, etc.

full ASCII: all of the 128 ASCII (American Standard Code for Information Interchange) characters, as opposed to half ASCII, an abbreviated code of only the first 96 characters.

full-duplex operation: a mode of information transmission in which data are transferred in both directions simultaneously, as opposed to a half-duplex or one-way operation. *See* **half-duplex operation.**

fully formed character: a solid character similar to one produced by a typewriter, as opposed to a dot-matrix or a seven-segment LED character.

function key: a special key on a computer terminal keyboard that, when pressed, causes a particular action or operation to be performed. On a word processor, some keys are dedicated (MOVE, ERASE, etc.) while others are user-defined (F1, F2, for example).

G

gap: an unrecorded length of magnetic tape or the time it takes for it to pass the read/write head. *See* **interblock gap; interrecord gap.**

gap character: (British): a character inserted into a string for a nondata use, such as a parity bit for error detection.

gap length: in tapes and other longitudinal recording media, the distance between recorded segments measured along the direction of the tape travel.

garbage: 1: (slang): worthless computer input or output data, especially output. The best-known expression in the computer world is "garbage in, garbage out." 2: obsolete data in a computer storage or program that just takes up memory space and should be removed.

garble: to transmit data that arrive at the receiving end in an unintelligible jumble, usually due to line noise or equipment malfunction.

Gbyte: an abbreviation for a gigabyte, 1 billion bytes. A byte is 8 bits.

general-purpose computer: a digital computer designed to handle any type of problem within its limitations of time, speed, and memory size. Its opposite is the dedicated computer, tailored to one specific application, such as the control of an industrial process by a fixed program.

generating program: a generator.

generator: anything that produces an output. In the computer world, a hardware clock generator and a software report generator are examples.

gigahertz: 1 billion hertz (cycles per second); 1000 megahertz, 1 million kilohertz.

GIGO: garbage in, garbage out, a data-processing truism. A $5 million mainframe computer solution is only as accurate as the entered data allow it to be, even with 36-bit double-precision processing.

GKS: *See* **Graphics Kernel System.**

GKS graphics package: a graphics software package conforming to the GKS (Graphics Kernel System) standard. *See* **Graphics Kernel System.**

glitch: an undesired voltage spike or transient in a digital system. A glitch appears about as often as the Loch Ness monster and is every bit as difficult to identify and eliminate.

global: describing a constant, variable, or other program parameter defined in the main body of a program and usable without further definition in all subroutines, procedures, and subprograms, as opposed to a local constant,

Graph **99**

variable, or other parameter defined in one unique program segment and usable only there.

global search: a search that the computer will conduct across page or window boundaries.

global substitution: in word processing, the substitution of one word or phrase for another everywhere it appears in an entire file, even across page boundaries.

global variable: a variable that is defined in any procedure or subroutine, as opposed to a local variable, which is defined in only one specific procedure.

GND: a common abbreviation for ground or ground potential, the zero-voltage condition. *See* **ground**.

grab a file: In Apple Computer's Lisa systems, to open a file by superimposing the cursor over the file's icon with the mouse and then pushing a button. A window opens on the CRT when the file is grabbed. *See* **mouse; window**.

grammar: in compilers, a description of the syntax or construction rules of a high-level language.

grandfather: describing a disk or file that has been copied, creating son copies, and at least one of the sons has been copied, creating a new son copy, making the old son a father and the old father a grandfather. Since any or all copies may be modified over a period of time, son, father, and grandfather are probably not identical copies, but bear only a family resemblance.

graph: a diagram showing the relationship between two variables in a rectangular coordinate system. Usually, the independent variable is drawn along the bottom (abscissa), and the dependent variable is scaled off vertically. The figure on the following page is a line graph. *See* **bar graph** and **pie chart** for other graph presentations.

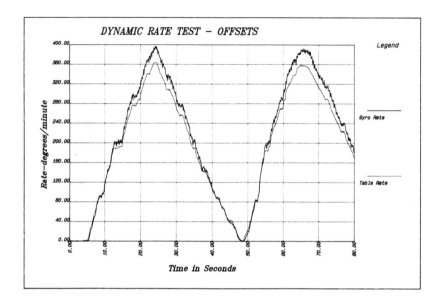

graphic: 1: giving a clear and descriptive picture of an event or a set of data. 2: pertaining to the use of diagrams, graphs, mathematical curves, etc., to express data.

graphics: the art and technics of drawing, particularly as practiced in science and engineering.

graphics board: a graphics-interface printed-circuit (PC) board installed or to be installed in an expansion-card slot to add graphics capability to a computer that was purchased without it.

graphics-display controller chip: an LSI chip that handles graphics-display address generation, freeing a host computer from the task.

graphics engine: the dedicated graphics processor, its operating system software, graphics memory, memory controller, and buffers, D/A converters, and CRT circuitry. A total graphics system consists of a large host computer, applications software, and the graphics engine.

graphics generator: a dedicated processor in a computer graphics system. It frees the host computer from purely graphics tasks. Synonymous with graphics engine. *See* **graphics system.**

Graphics Kernel System (GKS): an emerging graphics interface standard, supplanting the older Core standard. GKS was originated by DIN (Deutsches Institut für Normung) and attempts to achieve some standardization of graphics computers to allow intercommunication, software portability, common peripherals, etc.

graphics primitive: a simple line drawing, curve, or elementary closed figure that is used as a building block to create more complicated graphics forms and shapes. Primitives include straight line segments, arcs, circles, polygons, etc.

graphics-screen dump: a 1:1 mapping of the CRT screen to a hard-copy printer, which prints the screen's display of text and/or graphics exactly as it appears.

graphics system: a computer system optimized for graphics processing. No matter how complex it is, each system has a host computer containing the basic data to be processed, a display controller, and a display device.

graphics tablet: a synonym for a **data tablet,** a computer graphics input device. *See* **data tablet.**

graphics terminal: a computer terminal particularly designed and constructed for use in graphics systems. It will probably have a higher screen resolution than a normal data terminal, may have special graphics keys, and is likely to be a color CRT.

gray scale: in black-and-white graphics, the range of tints from pure white to pure black. In bit-mapped graphics, gray-scale resolution is a function of the number of bit planes; with eight planes, 2^8 or 256 different shades of gray can be displayed.

ground: the zero-voltage condition; usually, the reference from which all system voltages are measured.

group mark: a nondata character that denotes the end of a group of data characters in secondary storage.

hacker: a computer enthusiast or hobbyist. It is not derogatory at all. A dedicated hacker would rather compute than eat or sleep.

half-duplex channel: a communications channel that supports equipment at each of its ends, both of which can send or receive (but not both at the same time). Each station must take turns using the channel.

half-duplex operation: a data-transmission operating mode in which data can be transmitted in both directions, but in only one direction at a time. It cannot be sent simultaneously in both directions, as in full-duplex operation.

halt: 1: to cause a computer to stop its program run at a particular program instruction or statement or on command. 2: a noun describing such a stop in a program run.

halt button: a front-panel push-button switch on some computers. Pushing the button will cause the computer to stop running after completing its current instruction. It is used primarily during program development or under emergency conditions; sometimes it is labeled STOP.

handler: short for handler routine.

handler routine: a software routine through which a CPU communicates with and controls the operation of one or more of its peripheral devices connected to the system I/O bus. *Example:* a handler for a printer. The more popular term is I/O driver.

handshake: a communications protocol preceding transmission, in which signals are exchanged, requesting use of the channel, acknowledging the request, and granting it. Handshaking avoids loss of data due to unexpected transmissions.

hands on: pertaining to training courses in which the student uses the actual equipment (or a reasonable facsimile thereof) to gain practical, operating experience.

hanging indent: in typesetting, an indenting scheme in which the first line is set flush left and subsequent lines are indented by the same fixed amount of space, quantitatively expressed in picas.

hang-up: a programmed or unprogrammed stop during a program run, usually unprogrammed. Sometimes a small tight loop is used intentionally to hang up the computer to allow troubleshooting of the external hardware.

hard: computerese for permanent. *Examples:* hard disk, hard error, hard-sectored.

hard-copy printout: data produced by a computer-controlled printer on paper that can be retained for future reference, as opposed to data displayed on LEDs and other indicating lights, video monitors, TV tubes, etc., that are lost when updated or when power is turned off.

hard disk: a nonvolatile secondary or bulk memory-storage medium in the form of a nonflexible metallic disk coated with a magnetic oxide material. It is called a hard disk to distinguish it from the smaller flexible floppy disks used for the same purpose.

hard-disk controller: the electronics required to control the drive motion of a hard-disk drive and to decode, encode, read, and write data to/from the disk. In addition, it detects and corrects errors and converts formats of data going to and from it. One-chip VLSI disk controllers are on the market.

hard error: in magnetic recording, an error created when an attempt is made to write data into an area of the magnetic medium containing a physical flaw, such as lack of magnetic oxide material, and that no amount of backing up and of rewriting the data will cure. Contrast with a soft error, which can be corrected by a rewrite. Any other permanent error would be considered a hard error, as opposed to a correctable soft error.

hard hyphen: in word processing, a hyphen that is not inserted to break a line and will always be inserted in a word and always at the same place in it. *Example:* as in Saxe-Coburg. Contrast this with the soft hyphen, which a word processor inserts in a word to break it at the end of a line and which may appear at a different place in the word if the line is re-formed and falls differently at the end.

hard-sectored: pertaining to a hard or floppy disk in which the sector areas are delimited by "sector holes" through the disk, as opposed to soft-sectored disks in which the sector size and physical recording area on the disk are determined by software. *See* **sector.**

hard space: in word processing, a space inserted in a line by the writer and remains in the text at the same place regardless of how the line may be re-formed, as opposed to a soft space, which is added by the computer during justification and which may move if and when the line is re-formed.

hardware: a general technical term for the physical part of an electronic, hydraulic, mechanical, computer, or other system, as opposed to the software part (drawings, specifications, documentation, programs, test procedures, etc.). Hardware includes the metal, electronics, glass, wire, etc., which generally are permanent (hard). Software is flexible and subject to change (soft).

hash: 1: data with no mathematical or logical relationship. 2: electrical noise (interference) generated by commutators, motors, vibrators, etc., and super-imposed on a desired signal.

hash index: the initial predicted position of a data item in a hashed table.

hashing: a programming technique used to speed up the search for a data element in a table by making its position in the table dependent on the value of the data item. Hashing is sometimes called key-to-address transformation. Instead of searching the table to determine the address of a particular item, an attempt is made to calculate the address with the key.

hashing function: the procedure that produces the hash index in a hashed table of data items. *See* **hash index.**

hash total: a check sum of all the values in a specified field of a file, used for error detection or some other purpose, but otherwise having no mathematical significance. *Example:* a hash total of employee clock numbers.

hatch: in computer graphics, short for crosshatch, an area-fill technique.

head: 1: an electromagnetic device that reads, writes, or erases data on a magnetic storage unit, such as a disk, tape, cartridge, or cassette drive assembly. 2: a print head.

head crash: the disaster that happens when a magnetic-disk read/write head accumulates enough dirt, wear particles, dust, smoke, or other foreign matter to contact the magnetic oxide surface of a disk, resulting in major mayhem to recorded data. The head normally rides a few microinches above the disk surface on a cushion of air.

header: 1: the portion of a tape or disk file that contains identifying information for the group of recorded records. For tape that requires sequential access, the header is usually near the beginning of the tape, as the name implies. 2: the lines of text at the top of a page.

head gap: the air cushion on which the read/write head of a disk drive rides. The size of the gap is only a few microns, very much smaller than the diameter of a human hair. A zero head gap constitutes a head crash, when the head actually contacts the magnetic oxide surface (a real disaster).

HELP screen: a feature of many user-friendly computer software programs. When the command word HELP is entered on the keyboard, a hierarchy of menus is displayed on the CRT screen. Information on how to use the program and its commands is presented. The HELP screen data is usually more current than the user's manual.

hertz: a unit of frequency equal to one cycle per second (cps). Its abbreviation is Hz. Typical household electrical power is 60 Hz. The audible frequency band is about 20 to 16,000 Hz, depending on one's ears.

heuristic: the professional word for an educated trial-and-error solution for a problem.

hidden-surface removal: synonymous with clipping, in computer graphics.

hide: in some word processors, to remove control character symbols and soft spaces from a CRT displayed line in order for the operator to visualize how it will appear on the printed page. *Example:* soft hyphens are hidden on command.

hiding blocks: in word processing, hiding the markers that delimit a block of text. Hiding also makes the markers inoperable.

hierarchal structure: another name for a tree structure. A structure involving a hierarchy. In a hierarchal structure, all logic connections branch from the root node, and no connections are allowed to loop back on themselves.

hierarchy: a widely used word meaning an ordering of items, organizations, etc., according to importance or rank. *Example:* a computer program can be structured in a top-down modular hierarchy, as represented by the following figure:

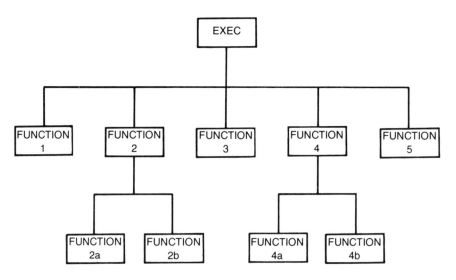

A MODULAR HIERARCHY

HIPO: hierarchy plus input, process, and output; an IBM documentation technique.

histogram: a bar graph in which each bar (usually vertical) represents the value of a single data item.

hit: in information retrieval, the successful end of a search; the matching of a stored data item with the search key(s).

Hollerith card: the familiar 80-column cardboard card, punched with rectangular holes of data to be read by a card reader for input to a computer. Hollerith cards are becoming obsolescent due to their bulk, slow speed of operation, and competition from magnetic disks and other secondary storage devices. Hollerith cards are more likely to be called IBM cards in this country.

Hollerith code: the code used to represent data on the punched cardboard cards known as Hollerith cards or IBM cards, invented by Dr. Herman Hollerith in 1888 for use with automatic textile looms. Each of the 80 vertical columns represents one alphabetic, numeric, or special punctuation character. *See* **Hollerith card**.

hologram: an optical three-dimensional recording technology emerging as an ultra-high-density storage mechanization for digital data. An image is recorded on a photographic film surface by splitting a laser beam to create an optical interference. The image is then recovered and refocused on the film.

home: the starting position for the video terminal cursor, at the far left-hand end of the first line at the top of the screen.

home computer: a loosely defined term for a small computer designed for the home market, without disk drives or printer, and usually costing less than $500. Such computers are normally designed for use with a TV as the video display, but most have optional CRT monitors. *Examples:* Commodore VIC-20, Atari 800, Radio Shack Color Computer.

hook: 1: a built-in expansion capability usually in software. *Example:* if a system has the hooks for a multitasking operating system, it can easily be added to enhance system operation at any time. 2: a link in a compiled high-level program (such as FORTRAN-80) to an imbedded program in an assembly language. *Example:* a user's driver module for an I/O device.

host computer: a larger computer used to enter and run an assembler, compiler, emulator, or simulator program for another, usually smaller, computer.

hub: the mounting hole in the center of a reel of ½-inch magnetic tape. The hub slides over the capstan in the tape-drive mechanism.

hub hole: the spindle hole in a floppy disk.

hyphen: a short line or dash used to connect two parts of a compound word (such as attorney-at-law) or to break a word at the end of a printed line.

hyphenate: to join with a hyphen.

hyphenation: the splitting of a word at the end of a typed or printed line in accordance with an established rule or algorithm, adding a hyphen to terminate the line. Synonymous with hyphenization.

hyphen help: a feature of MicroPro's WordStar word-processing program. When a paragraph is re-formed with hyphen help ON, the computer will find any long words that almost fit at the end of a line but had to be moved down the next line, leaving an undesirably large space. It will then test the word to see if it has two or more syllables, decide where to break the word, move the cursor there, and then stop. You then decide if you want to hyphenate or not.

hyphenization: a synonym for hyphenation.

hyphenize: a synonym for hyphenate.

Hz: hertz, the international unit of frequency, equal to one cycle per second.

I

icon: a small graphical symbol used by Apple's Lisa computer (and some others) as a mnemonic to show what programs and data files are available.

identifier: a name, symbol, or label, preferably a mnemonic, given to an entity, such as a significant address or a variable, in a computer program.

IF-THEN-ELSE (or IFTHENELSE): one of the three basic building blocks of structured programming.

ignore: to inhibit or to skip the processing of a given datum.

ignore character: a control character inserted in a block of data to cause the processor to ignore one or more data items, perhaps known to be erroneous. Synonymous with error and erase characters.

image: 1: an exact copy of a program, procedure, or routine but stored on a different medium, such as tape instead of disk. 2: the output of a linker, which processes one or more object modules to create an executable program.

impact printer: a printer that prints when the appropriate key strikes an inked ribbon against the paper, as opposed to one using other principles of operation, such as heat.

increment: 1: to increase an amount by adding a small integer, usually 1. 2: the amount of the increase.

incremental spacing: an ability of some printers to move their print heads small fractions of a normal character space, both horizontally and vertically (some as little as 1/120 inch horizontally; for a 12-pitch character font, 10 incremental movements per inch are therefore possible). These printers provide boldface text by printing the text to be emphasized once, backing up to the first character plus one increment, and reprinting it a second time, one increment to the right for all characters to be boldface.

indent, indentation: to improve the readability of a computer program listing by increasing the left margin (leading spaces) of associated sections of code or pseudocode, such as a FOR-NEXT loop or a subprogram.

Example:

```
FOR  I = 1 TO 10
     INPUT A,B
     IF A = B THEN 120
     A = A + 1
NEXT  I
```

Structured languages, such as PASCAL, use indenting as a mandatory, functional requirement.

index: 1: a pointer or indicator: one points with the index finger. 2: a quantitative, measurable indicator used in business modeling and forecasting.

indexed sequential-access method (ISAM):   a file-access technique faster than the sequential-access method, probably the most used file-reading process, but slower than the random-access method, which requires more file space. ISAM records are stored in contiguous locations, as sequential files are, but the location is not determined by a record "key," as in the random-access method. In ISAM, special "prime" data records are stored together as a "physical record," the largest number of prime records that can be written into one sector, the elemental unit of storage on a disk. An "index" file, containing a pointer (address) to each physical record and the highest key value of any logic record within that physical record, is also stored on the disk. The index file usually is used only by the disk operating system, so the operation appears like random access to the user.

indexed sequential file: a disk file in which records are written sequentially with one or more search keys, which are recorded in an index. The files can then be processed randomly using the index.

index hole: a hole through a floppy disk and its jacket, near the spindle access hole in the center of the disk. The index hole marks the start of the first sector when detected by sensors within the disk-drive mechanism.

indexing slot: a slot in the card-edge connector of a printed-circuit card, cut in asymmetrically with respect to the center of the conductors, to prevent improper upside-down insertion of the card in its connector. A polarizing slot.

inferior number: in typesetting, a subscript. In the Intergraphics automatic typesetting system, a control code, i is inserted to indicate an inferior number, avoiding the time-wasting advance of the platen to type a subscript below the line. *Example:* a{i2} for a_2.

information: the meaning associated with a data item, using known conventions. *Example:* 2 is a data item; when February is assigned the value 2, as the second month of the year, then 2 becomes information in that context.

information channel: synonymous with data link.

information feedback: the retransmission of received data back to the transmitting station for the purpose of error checking.

information hiding: a software system development discipline. Information hiding is a design and coding technique that "conceals" or encapsulates complex data structures (e.g., stacks, arrays of strings, pointer structures) inside program modules. Only selected modules are allowed to use the concealed data structure. The information-hiding concept is attributed to Parnas.

information packet: a packet, a kernel of transmitted data of convenient size. *Example:* 1024 bytes with 144 bits of header. Packets may be sent in burst mode.

information theory: the mathematics defining the probability of accurate transmission of messages over a distance in the presence of noise, distortion, and equipment failures. Information theory started with a 1948 paper by Claude Shannon. Bell Labs leads the way.

informative prompt: a computer prompt that requires no operator action but provides some bit of information. *See* **prompt**.

inherent error: an error in current processing, but one that was generated in a previous operation and simply carried into the present one.

inhibit: 1: to disable. 2: to apply a signal to a device to prevent its operation.

initial condition: a necessary precondition, status, or value that must be established prior to the execution of a program or routine.

initialization: a process that sets all variables and constants in a program or routine to prescribed values at the beginning of a run (or at least checks that they are already correct) in order to assure proper execution.

initialize: 1: to perform whatever is necessary to start up a computer or one of its programs, such as resetting counters to their starting values, setting the program counter to the first instruction, resetting the interrupt flip-flop, etc. 2: to force a digital device into its starting state.

ink-jet printer: a printing technology using a print head that sprays dots of colored or black ink under computer control to form text characters or graphics images. (The Irwin/Olivetti JP101 printer sprays a fine powder instead of a fluid.) Ink-jet printers are quiet and highly reliable, with no moving parts.

in-line gun: in color CRTs, an arrangement of the red, green, and blue electron guns in which the center of the three electron beams lie on a straight line, as opposed to the delta gun configuration with the gun axes forming an equilateral triangle.

input: 1: a signal transmitted from a peripheral device to the CPU. Unless otherwise indicated, input or output is always with reference to the CPU. 2: a signal transmitted into any unit, circuit, or system. *See* **I/O port.**

input block: 1: an area of main memory reserved as a parking area for data as the data are first input from disk (or other secondary storage) prior to the data's assignment to working areas of memory. 2: a recorded block of data being moved into main memory or destined to be so soon.

input-limited: describing a processor, program, or condition in which the processing time is determined by the speed of much slower input devices; processing speed is limited to allow for the input of the required data. For most computers, this is the norm.

input/output devices: external peripheral hardware equipment used to enter (input) data into a computer or accept data from the computer (output) for display, storage, further processing, or transmission to other devices, including computers.

input/output library: the set of driver routines written to control the operation of a computer system's I/O devices.

input reader: (British): an input routine.

input routine: a subroutine or subprogram that implements the input of data from a given peripheral (I/O) device. Also called an I/O routine.

inquiry: a request for information by a computer or one of its peripherals; it often requires an immediate response.

inquiry character (ENQ): a teletypewriter control character used to request a response from the addressed receiving station.

inquiry display terminal: (British): a video terminal.

inquiry station: (British): a terminal used for the accessing of remote files.

INSERT: a word-processor and screen-editor command and mode, used to bring in additional characters, words, lines, or whole paragraphs into a body of text. Unlike an EXCHANGE or SUBSTITUTE command, INSERT adds the new material at the cursor, pushing the existing characters to the right. Sometimes the entries are keyed in; other times they are read in from stored files or archival data.

INSERT mode: *See* **INSERT.**

instancing: to perform transformations on an image defined in one place in order to reproduce the same image in another place in the field of view on a graphics screen.

instruction: 1: the basic elemental one-liner in a computer program that expresses a single direction or order of the programmer in a form the computer can understand and execute. 2: a program statement that specifies what operation is to be performed and the values of the operands, or at least their locations. A computer operates by executing sequentially a list of instructions that form a program. 3: the binary word into which the instruction is coded.

integrated circuit: an entire functional electronic circuit, digital or linear, fabricated on one tiny monolithic silicon chip, using various techniques. An integrated circuit may contain anywhere from a few to more than 30,000 transistors, resistors, diodes, capacitors, etc. The ultimate minimum size of integrated-circuit transistors will be measured in ångström units.

integrated software: an advanced feature of some computers, such as Apple Computer's Lisa, and advanced software, such as VisiCorp's Visi On™, that employ a "natural" desk-top approach. The key advantage is the ability to run, display, and transfer data simultaneously between several active programs, such as word processor, spreadsheet analysis, graphics, etc. The CRT screen is divided into two or more "windows" that can simultaneously display associated active programs; window size can be adjusted with keyboard commands. Data are moved from one window to another by moving the cursor with a mouse. *Example:* from a spreadsheet analysis, bottom-line figures could be moved directly into a pie-chart graphic. *See* **grab a file; mouse; open a window.**

integrated system: a combination of separate elements coordinated into a harmonious, compatible, interrelated whole.

intelligence: containing a microprocesor, in the computer sense. Artificial intelligence, however, implies some simulations of human brain capacities, such as the ability to learn or to reason deductively or intuitively.

intelligent copier: a computer or word-processing peripheral that acts as an automatic printer. No one has to go to the copier and manually insert an original; the document is transmitted directly from the word processor as serial data. The copier's microprocessor translates the data into character images transferred to paper by a xerographic process. Some have multiple character fonts and will sort and collate.

intelligent device: an equipment that contains a microprocessor or micro-computer programmed to process data right at the device, as opposed to a "dumb" device, which can only transmit or receive information to or from a computer.

intelligent terminal: one form of intelligent device, usually a CRT terminal that handles some data processing itself, without the help of the computer to which it is connected. It may also do some "preprocessing" of data before transmitting to the main computer. *Example:* a point-of-sale terminal. Synonymous with smart terminal.

interactive: describing a program, routine, procedure, or process that expects and responds to human intervention and interrelation with the computer. *See* **interactive routine**. Synonymous with conversational.

interactive routine: a computer program that prompts, accepts, and reacts to human operator inputs, runs intermittently, stops for new inputs, often with English language sentences, which give it a humanlike quality, reacts in response to those inputs, etc.; in effect, a semiautomatic mode of operation.

interactive simulator: a simulator program that runs as an interactive routine.

interblock gap (IBG): the length of unrecorded magnetic tape between two adjacent blocks of recorded data on a reel, cassette, or cartridge. Same as block gap.

interface: 1: a shared boundary. 2: the process of making two different devices (or people) work together successfully. 3: a piece of hardware designed to make two equipments compatible; an adapter. 4: describing such a piece of hardware (an interface board, module, box, card, etc.). 5: to solve the problems and do the design work necessary to interface people or equipment.

interface board, card, module: a hardware module that implements whatever is necessary to connect two different equipments or systems together and operate them successfully.

interference: the presence or the result of undesired noise signals in a communications channel or circuit.

interior label: the label written on a magnetic tape at its beginning to identify its contents or function, as opposed to the external sticker label on the reel container.

interlace: in raster-scan graphics, a "raster" is created by a "frame" of 525 horizontal lines drawn by the CRT's electron beam as two intermeshed alternating "fields" of 262 lines and 263 lines, respectively, with the lines of one field lying between (interlaced with) the lines of the second field. Every 1/60 second, each field is refreshed. Interlacing reduces the bandwidth (and therefore the expense) of associated electronics.

interlock: a hardware or software switch that, when actuated, prevents some other action or is prerequisite for another operation. An interlock switch on the back door of some electric equipment disconnects power when the door is opened, actuating the switch and preventing electric shock.

intermittent: 1: describing an equipment malfunction that comes and goes, like the loss of a signal due to a broken wire inside an unbroken sleeve of insulation, or a bad connection during vibration. 2: the interruption itself when this happens.

internal format: the form taken by data after they have been input into some device, implying that this form was altered when the data were entered.

internally stored program: one in main memory, as opposed to one on disk or some other form of secondary storage.

internal memory: the storage within the computer or the computer chip itself. Synonymous with internal storage.

internal storage: 1: with reference to a computer, its high-speed directly addressable main memory, usually semiconductor, as opposed to secondary storage on a magnetic disk or tape. 2: with respect to a single-chip micro-computer or processor, the memory located on the chip, as opposed to additional memory on other connected chips, cards, or boards.

interrecord gap (IRG):   an unrecorded length of magnetic tape between two records. Synonymous with interblock gap.

inverse video: a special feature used to highlight and emphasize selected words, phrases, lines, areas, etc., on a CRT display screen. If the normal presentation is light characters on a dark background, the areas of inverse video will display dark characters on a light background. Inverse video is programmable. Not all terminals have it.

invoking document: in word processing, synonymous with matrix or matrix document.

I/O: input/output. The abbreviation may refer to devices or operations. Sometimes it is a noun, but usually it is an adjective.

I/O buffer: a temporary storage register functioning as a buffer between the high-speed main memory and the much slower I/O devices. It prevents loss of data going in either direction and allows the processor to go about its other chores without waiting.

I/O cable: a cable connecting the CPU and an I/O device or connecting two peripherals.

I/O device: *See* **input/output devices**.

I/O port: an extension of the CPU data bus to the outside world; a set of terminals, one for each bit in the data word. Usually, the port has an associated latch for input and output data to and from the CPU and one of its peripheral units. The port may be in a RAM unit or a special I/O chip and will normally be assigned as either an input or an output. Usually, I/O ports are bidirectional, and port direction is defined during initialization of a given program. Sometimes I/O port directions are changed under CPU control during a program run.

ISAM: *See* **indexed sequential-access method**.

italics: a type style with characters that slant up and to the right. Italics are used for emphasis: to catch your eye. *These words are set in italics.*

item: a group of data characters having a common purpose.

item size: the number of characters comprising a unit of data.

iterate: 1: to repeat. 2: to execute a series of instructions in a loop until some exit condition tests true.

iteration: 1: one cycle of instructions in a loop. 2: an iterative process. 3: in structured code, the execution of the same basic block over and over again until a false condition becomes true (or a true condition becomes false).

J

jack: a two-conductor female connector, into which a male plug is inserted.

JCL: the abbreviation for job-control language.

jet printer: short for ink-jet printer.

job: a specified unit of work for a computer operating in the batch mode. The job package normally includes all necessary programs, linkages, files, and instructions to the operating system. Instructions may be written using job-control language (JCL).

job-control language (JCL): a programming language designed to facilitate the control of a computer operating in a batch process mode. *See* **job**.

jumper: a wire or cable, usually short or temporary, used to connect two points in an electrical circuit, often to correct an error but sometimes to modify or update a circuit board or to adapt it for a special purpose.

jumper-selectable: a term used to describe an equipment option that may be exercised by installing one or more short jumper wires between appropriate connecting points, usually on a printed-circuit card.

justify: 1: to adjust the position of printed characters on a page so that all lines have the desired length and both left- and right-hand margins are regular. 2: to shift the contents of a register so that the most significant or least significant digit is at some specified position in the register. 3: to align characters horizontally or vertically to fit positioning constraints of a format. *See* **left-justify**; **right-justify**.

K

K: kilo, the Greek prefix for 1000. A 1K resistor is 1000 ohms. But when used to define the size of a memory, an 8K memory is 8192 bytes, an integer power of 2 (2^{13}). A 64K memory is actually 65,536 bytes (2^{16}), or bits, for a RAM chip.

K-bit: short for kilobit, 1000 bits.

K-byte: short for kilobyte, 1000 bytes.

kern: 1: the part of a typeset letter character that projects beyond its side bearings. 2: to form or set with a kern. 3: to become kerned.

kernel: a small but essential part of something. *Example:* a program.

kerning: the squeezing of letters together.

key: 1: one or more characters in a data item used to identify it or to control its use. 2: one of the finger-actuated levers on a video terminal or typewriter keyboard.

keybar: the traditional old-fashioned typewriter lever, mechanically linked to a corresponding type key at one end and a type bar with an upper- and lower-case character at the other end. Keybars drive an inked ribbon onto the paper when the key is pressed, transferring the character to the paper.

keybar printer: an automatic impact printer employing keybars to strike the ribbon when the corresponding key is pressed. *See* **keybar**.

keyboard: a commonly used method for manual insertion of data into a computer; an integral part of any two-way terminal, such as a video (CRT) terminal or teletypewriter. Keyboards for terminals are quite similar to the familiar typewriter keyboard, with the alphanumeric and numeric keys in the same QWERTY places, but with extra special-function keys in both upper and lower cases.

keyboard file: in UCSD PASCAL software, KEYBOARD is the name of the nonechoing equivalent of the standard INPUT file.

keyboard scan: the periodic sampling of the switches actuated by the keys of a keyboard by the CPU to determine if a key has been pushed, and if so, which one.

keystroke: 1: the action of pressing one of the keys on a keyboard. 2: the result of such an action.

keyword: a command name, qualifier, or option predefined to the computer, which recognizes it and acts accordingly. When entered from a keyboard, the keywords must be typed exactly as defined in the operating system manual; the only exception is a valid truncation or abbreviation.

kHz: kilohertz (1000 cycles per second), a unit of frequency.

kill: 1: to delete lines or characters from a program during text editing. 2: to stop an operation. *Example:* a spool kill command to stop a spooling operation.

kilo-: a prefix from the Greek, meaning 1000 of anything. A kilogram is 1000 grams.

kilobit: 1000 bits.

kilobytes: 1000 bytes.

L

label: one or more letters and numbers or a symbol used to tag a program statement or instruction in a program listing, usually the entry to a loop or subroutine. The use of labels in lieu of statement numbers saves time and avoids errors when program steps are added; this would otherwise require the re-numbering of many statements.

label field: the first column on the left in the listing of an assembly-language program; the field reserved for any label assigned to a program statement:

Example:

Label	Mnemonic	Operand	Comment
ALPHA	LDAA	#23	;Load 23 into ACC A

label record: an identification record near the start of a file stored on a magnetic disk, containing information about the contents and format of the file.

language: a set of symbols with commonly understood and agreed meanings when used in a predefined manner by a number of people who can thus communicate with one another.

laser printing: an extremely high-speed printing method that burns character images onto a rotating drum with a laser beam. The heated surface area picks up toner that is then offset to paper. Character quality is very high; so is the price. Laser printing can be used as a photocomposer output and is completely computer compatible.

last in, first out (LIFO):   a queue servicing process in which the first to be serviced is the last one to be added to the queue; this is the LIFO method used in microcomputer program stack operations.

LCD: *See* **liquid-crystal display.**

leader: the blank section of tape at the beginning of a reel, cassette, or cartridge of magnetic tape. It may not even have the magnetic oxide coating.

leadered line: a line that has been filled out with a character, such as a period or dash. *Example:*

-- FOLD HERE --

leadering: filling out a line with a character, such as an asterisk or dash; justifying the line with the character.

leading (pronounced ledding):   the space between two lines of type, measured in units called "points" (72 points = 1 inch). It came from hot-lead typesetting technology when lead bars were actually inserted between lines of type to separate them.

leading zero: any zero that precedes the most significant nonzero digit of a number, generally to fill out a constant width data field.

leased line: a dedicated phone line used for telecommunications, as opposed to the ordinary voice-grade line used with a modem and acoustic coupler.

LED: light-emitting diode, a commonly used alphanumeric display device that glows when supplied with a specified current. The most common color is red, but others are yellow and green.

left-justified: the term "justify" comes from the printing art, where it means to make a line of type fit exactly into a desired length, such as the width of a column. In computer use, it refers to the way the computer will interpret the empty spaces in a data field of numbers not having the same number of digits. If the data field and the numbers are left-justified, the computer will enter the MSD in the leftmost space and fill in the field as necessary with trailing zeros. *Example:* given the following data list, 1.5, 1.001, 23.4567, 0.0991, assume an 8-bit data word. If left-justified, the computer will interpret the data as follows for an 8-digit data field:

```
1 . 500000
1 . 001000
23 . 45670
0 . 099100
```

left-justify: 1: to adjust the printing positions for characters on a page to make the left margin even. In the computer sense, to shift the contents of a shift register until the most significant digit is at a predefined position in the register. 2: to align characters horizontally in order to place the leftmost character of a string in a specified position.

leg: one path in a branching routine or procedure.

length: the number of bits in a word, character, record, message, or any other data element.

letter out: (British): erase.

letter quality: describing the print quality achieved with fully formed characters vs. dot-matrix letters and numbers. Letter-quality printers are more expensive.

letter-quality printer: a printer with a fully formed character set. Sometimes you see "correspondence quality."

librarian: a software utility program in some operating systems (OS). Librarian works in conjunction with the linker/loader utility to retrieve other OS utilities and user-program modules from a disk or other secondary storage and dispatches them for linking.

library: a collection of subroutines, procedures, and programs written for a given computer and saved for future use.

library routine: a tested, debugged routine saved in hard copy and/or on magnetic media for later use in new programs under development.

LIFO: *See* **last in, first out.**

light-emitting diode: the full name for an LED, but hardly anyone uses it.

light pen: a computer input device used in conjunction with a CRT video terminal. A penlike housing containing a small photocell with a photomultiplier is held against the face or screen of the CRT. When the electron beam passes directly under the pen point, a coincidence pulse is generated to identify to the computer that particular point on the screen. Light pens are used extensively in CAD/CAM work.

line: 1: a conducting wire between equipment. 2: synonymous with cable.

linear: 1: describing a device that operates in a proportional or continuous manner, such as an analog amplifier. Not discrete, discontinuous, or digital, but analog. 2: having straight-line properties.

linear PI: *See* **PI** (programmed instruction).

line-at-a-time printer: (British): a line printer.

line driver: an amplifier that transmits digital signals over a line, from one device to another. Line drivers are almost always used if the devices are located in different equipment separated by a distance of more than 18 inches or so. Usually, a line driver has a single input and a two-wire output; one wire carries the digital variable, the other its complement. The two wires are twisted together and covered with a braided-wire shield to minimize noise-voltage pickup. A line receiver is used at the other end of the line. *See* **line receiver.**

line editor: a software program used to correct errors in another program or text on a line-by-line basis. The line to be changed is placed into an edit buffer first. Then it may be altered using predefined edit commands. *See* **screen editor.**

line feed or line-feed: 1: to advance a printer or the CRT cursor from one line to the next line. 2: short for the line-feed character.

line-feed character: a nonprinting control character transmitted by a computer to a printer or video terminal to cause the cursor (and with it the line where ensuing characters are printed) to move to the next line.

line-feed code: a synonym for the line-feed control character.

line drawing: an illustration done entirely in lines, with gradations in tone and shade implemented by variations in line width, intensity, spacing, etc.

line illustration: synonymous with line drawing.

line noise: any unwanted voltage coupled capacitively or induced electro-magnetically into an information-carrying transmission line or a power-supply line. The undesired noise voltage adds to the data signal, degrading or even obliterating it.

line of code: one line in a program listing, either assembly language or high-level language (HLL). One line in an HLL is more properly called a program statement.

line printer: a computer peripheral device that prints an entire line of char-acters simultaneously, as opposed to a serial or character printer that prints only one character at a time. A line printer is a high-speed printer.

line receiver: a differential amplifier commonly used at the receiving end of a twisted shielded pair of wires carrying a digital signal between two equipments separated by a distance of more than a few inches. Usually, the line receiver has two inputs and a signal output; it receives the digital variable on one input and its complement on the other from a compatible line driver. *See* **line driver.**

line spacing: the number of lines per inch of text. Spacing may be single, one and a half, double, or triple, as in typewriters, as well as half for subscripts and superscripts. Standard single spacing is six lines per inch; double spacing is three lines per inch.

line transient: a voltage fluctuation of short duration, usually milliseconds, but sometimes in the microsecond range. Line transients are noise. They can result in errors and other problems in digital equipment not properly designed to prevent them or unprotected by filters or line-noise-suppression equipment.

link: 1: a data-transmission channel. *Example:* a two-way digital data link. 2: the part of a subroutine, subprogram, or procedure that connects it into the mainline code. 3: the process of joining together two or more separate programs into an integrated whole. 4: to use a linker utility.

liquid-crystal display (LCD):   an electroluminescent display used in calculators and some portable computers, favored because of its low power requirements, flat profile, and relatively low price. Most digital watches have LCD faces.

LISP: List Processor, a high-level programming language used by computer professionals for artificial intelligence research. LISP was the brainchild of John McCarthy of Stanford, while still at MIT in the early 1960s. It uses lists as the only data structure. *See* **list.**

list: 1: an ordered set of data items. 2: to cause a computer printer to print out a program or data. 3: the printout or listing.

listening on the bus: describing an equipment connected electrically to a computer bus system and in a state in which it can receive messages sent to it and respond to them. It may be passive most of the time.

listing: a program list, a computer printout of a list of statement numbers, statements, object codes, data, errors, etc., for a program or a part of it.

literal: 1: a word, number, or symbol that names, identifies, or defines itself literally and does not represent something else figuratively. *Example:* the constant TWO in an assembly-language listing is literal if it stands for the number 2. 2: short for a string literal, as opposed to a string variable. A string literal is a string constant. *Example:* the string HELLO, HOW ARE YOU? is a string literal. A$ is a string variable in BASIC. One value of A$ might be HELLO, HOW ARE YOU?

load: to input data or programs into a computer, one of its registers, or one of its peripheral devices.

loader: a generic term for software that performs loading. It may be a program that loads other programs from an external bulk-storage device; it may be short for a linker/loader.

loading: the process of entering a file into a text or screen editor, an interpreter, compiler, or another processing software program.

loading error: an error introduced when a program is loaded into the computer from an I/O storage device. For most computers this is a rare event. If not, do something.

loading routine: a loader.

load module: 1: a software utility that performs linkage and relocation when run; a linker/loader. 2: a computer-ready object module.

load point: a preset point near the beginning-of-tape marker (BOT) at which a magnetic tape that has just been placed on a tape transport will be positioned. The BOT marker is downreel from the physical end of the tape, and the load point is downreel from the BOT.

local network: short for local area network (LAN), the system that interconnects computers and workstations within one building (or, at most, a group of buildings in one place). *Examples:* Xerox's EtherNET, Datapoint's ARCnet.

logged disk: a floppy disk that has been logged. *See* **logging a disk**.

logged drive: a drive containing a disk that has been logged in. This is sloppy terminology; it is the disk that has to be logged in, not the drive. *See* **logging a disk**.

logging a disk: identifying to the computer's operating system that a new disk has been inserted into a given disk drive. An operating system software maintains an internal record (bit map) of the unused (and therefore available) sectors on all disk drives. Whenever a disk is changed, the new disk must be "logged in" by typing a Control C (or whatever your system specifies). The computer will then make a new bit map for this disk and write to the available empty sectors. If the disk is not logged in, the computer thinks the old disk is still there and will improperly write to the new one. Logging in is necessary only when inserting a new disk, not when merely changing the current drive.

logical record: a collection of items independent of their physical environment. Portions of the same logical record may be located in different physical records.

logic-seeking printer: a printer that advances to the first actual print position on the next line, after a line-feed, rather than starting at the left margin. In printing headings, columnar data, etc., speed is materially increased.

login or log-in: 1: the sequence of keystroke commands, responses, and other computer terminal interactions required by a particular computer's operating-system software to establish a user's communication with it. 2: to perform the required keystrokes.

LOGO: a programming language for introducing computer concepts to children. It is not an acronym or abbreviation—merely a name given to it by Wallace Feurzeig, of Bolt, Beranek and Newman, Incorporated, one of the developers of the language. The principal authors were the LOGO group at MIT, under the direction of Seymour Papert. The name is derived from the Greek "logikos," of reason. *See* **turtle; turtle geometry; turtle graphics**.

longitudinal-redundancy-check character (LRCC): on a tape where each character is represented in a lateral row of bits, a character used for checking the parity of each track in the longitudinal direction. Such a character is usually the last one recorded in each block. It is used in some magnetic recording systems to reestablish the initial recording status. Sometimes the abbreviation is LRC.

longitudinal-redundancy checking (LRC): an error-detection technique implemented by adding a longitudinal-redundancy-check character to a block of recorded data. *See* **longitudinal-redundancy-check character**.

long-persistence phosphor: in cathode-ray tubes, a phosphor material that emits photons for a longer period after the excitation source (the electron beam of the electron gun) is removed, as compared with normal-persistence phosphors. Persistence is a function of the material used in the screen coating.

look-up table: an area in memory set aside for a table of values that are simply fetched when needed, and not calculated with a mathematical equation or algorithm. *Example:* a table of trigonometric sine values stored in lieu of computing their values using a series expansion.

look-up table (word processing): a keyboard layout chart of standard character keys vs. special character keys (math, Greek, Arabic, etc.).

loop: 1: a sequence of computer instructions executed again and again until an exit condition is satisfied. 2: a primitive construct of structured programming.

loop check: the echoing of transmitted data back to the sender for comparison with the original, for the detection of transmission errors.

looping: describing a computer or program that has entered and is executing a loop. Sometimes it is unintentional.

LSI: large-scale integration, usually about 1000 or more gates on a single integrated-circuit chip.

LSI-intensive board: a hardware board with a high percentage of large-scale integrated circuits.

luminance: the luminous intensity of a surface in a given direction per unit of projected area.

luminous: reflecting or radiating light.

M

mA: milliampere, one thousandth of an ampere, a unit of electric current.

machine: an apparatus of interrelated parts with separate functions used to perform some kind of work. Loosely, the computer.

machine error: an error caused by a hardware failure in the computer or one of its peripherals (very rare compared with software blunders).

machine-independent: pertaining to a language, procedure, process, program, etc., that is not dependent on the unique characteristics of a given computer system. Machine independence is hard to find, but the industry is always striving to reach that goal, particularly in high-level languages.

machine instruction: a machine-language instruction.

machine language: a computer instruction or program expressed directly in a binary code that the machine understands. All other programming languages, such as assembly (symbolic or mnemonic) language and the high-level languages (BASIC, FORTRAN, PL/M, etc.), must be translated into the binary machine languages, usually by computers using assembler, interpreter, or compiler language-translation software programs.

machine-oriented: pertaining to any language, procedure, program, process, etc., that is dependent on the unique characteristics of one particular computer system. *Example:* all assembly languages are machine-oriented. The opposite is machine-independent.

magnetic disc: *See* **magnetic disk**.

magnetic disk: a flat, circular plate with a recording surface of magnetic material on which computer data can be stored by selective magnetization of the material. Magnetic-disk equipment falls into two major categories: hard disks, used with the larger systems, and flexible disks or floppies.

magnetic drum: a nearly obsolete form of magnetic bulk storage. Data are stored in cylindrical tracks on a drum cylinder rotating at high speeds. Access speeds are intermediate between those for magnetic core and hard disks. One military aircraft simulator uses two drum memories for high-speed intermediate storage of simulated radar map data. But applications are getting scarce.

magnetic field: a condition of space, appearing as a force on a moving charge or a magnetic pole within that space in the vicinity of a magnet or any current-carrying material.

magnetic head: a small electromagnet used to read, record, or erase data on a magnetic medium. The head is installed in a tape-drive mechanism along the line of tape travel, where the tape must pass immediately over its surface.

magnetic-ink character: a printer character of ink containing magnetic particles that can be detected and recognized by magnetic-ink character recognition (MICR) equipment.

magnetic polarity: *See* **magnetic pole**.

magnetic pole: the region of a magnet into which the magnetic lines of flux converge and enter (a south pole) or from which the flux lines emanate and diverge (a north pole).

magnetic tape: a plastic tape (mag tape), usually ¼ inch wide for cartridges and ½ inch wide for tape transports, coated with a magnetic material, used with a tape-drive mechanism for bulk storage of computer data, files, and programs. When required, the data are transferred (read) into main memory for use by the processor unit during program execution. *See* **cartridge**; **magnetic-tape transport**; **tape cassette**. Data read from magnetic tape are not destroyed (unless someone or something goofs) and may be used over and over again. Reading from or writing to magnetic tape is done under program control by the CPU.

magnetic-tape deck: the electromechanical mechanism that handles magnetic tape, moving the tape from the supply reel past the read/write and erase heads to the take-up reel. It includes the read/write electronics and suitable control switches and indicators. Synonymous with magnetic-tape drive, tape deck, tape drive, and magnetic-tape unit.

magnetic-tape drive: *See* **magnetic-tape deck.**

magnetic-tape format: the format in which data are recorded on magnetic tape, usually in accordance with some standard defining block length, gaps, etc.

magnetic-tape transport: a computer-controlled tape drive mechanism that transfers magnetic tape from one large (7-inch diameter, for example) reel to another, running the tape past a read/write head, which converts the information into electrical pulses that can be input into a computer. *See* **magnetic tape.**

magnitude: in mathematics, the absolute value of a quantity, without regard to its sign. The magnitude of either $+2$ or -2 is 2.

mag tape: short for magnetic tape.

mainframe: 1: a computer chassis in which the component printed-circuit (PC) cards or boards are housed. 2: a high-speed computer, larger, faster, and more expensive than high-end minicomputers. *Example:* an IBM 370. A Cray-1 might be overdoing it. The boundary between a small mainframe and a super-mini is fuzzy indeed.

mainline program: the set of instructions that the computer executes sequentially, usually just once during a given program. When the program branches to a subroutine, it has left the mainline program.

main memory: the portion of a computer memory that can be directly accessed by its address registers, as opposed to its mass or bulk memory, such as magnetic-disk, -tape, or -cassette storage. Main memory uses either high-speed semiconductors (ROM, PROM, and RAM) or magnetic cores in the older, obsolescent machines.

main storage: synonymous with main memory.

maintainability: the ease with which a software program or a hardware system can be fixed or restored to working order when bugs are discovered or failures occur during the lifetime of the program or equipment.

maintenance: the phase in the life cycle of a software program or system following its development, testing, installation, and final acceptance. Maintenance costs usually outrun acquisition costs, particularly in large projects, both software and hardware.

makeup: the design and layout of text, artwork, headers, footers, page numbers, etc., for a document page. Also called page composition and paste-up.

Manchester code: one of several self-clocking binary codes, in which the information is in the direction of the phase (polarity) change that occurs in the middle of each bit time. Synonymous with phase encoding. *Example:* Manchester II and Manchester II+180.

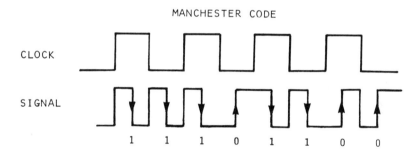

MANCHESTER CODE

CLOCK

SIGNAL

1   1   1   0   1   1   0   0

Manchester II code: *See* **Manchester code.**

Manchester II+180 code: the same as Manchester II code except that a digital 1 is associated with the opposite polarity change.

manual entry: the input of data to the computer, usually through the keyboard, but it could be by means of switches, light pens, or optical character readers as long as a human hand is involved.

manual input: 1: synonymous with manual entry. 2: data entered manually. 3: a device used for manual entry of data or programs.

manual mode: a computer operational mode in which all automatic features are turned off and the computer is implemented to receive its commands from the front panel.

manuscript: the original document prepared by an author.

margin: the white space from the edge of the paper to the nearest edge of the first (or last) character in each line. In 80-character lines, standard margins are 10 characters wide.

marginal test: (British): a test to determine the operating limits of an equipment. *Example:* to establish the margins of safety of the equipment.

mark: binary 1 in early teletypewriter digital communications. Binary 0 was called a space.

marking: *See* **text marking**.

mask: an electronic form on a word-processor screen containing blank fields to be filled in by the operator. *Example:* the mask for a sales letter would have fields for the name, address, title, etc., of the recipient.

massage data: (slang): to further refine or process it.

mass storage: 1: synonymous with bulk storage. 2: a memory having a large capacity (usually in the megabytes), connected to a computer's I/O bus and under its control, such as a magnetic-disk drive or tape-cassette drive, in which programs and data, not in active use, can be stored for retrieval and later use within a few seconds or less.

master clock: the heartbeat of the computer from which all timing pulses are derived to control the sequence of events within the machine. The basic reference is usually a piezoelectric crystal oscillator whose very stable output is amplified to increase its power and then is "counted down" or divided in frequency to provide outputs with the required periods.

master file: a file directory that references and lists all the other files in a file system.

master library tape: a reel of magnetic tape containing all the programs and the subroutine library for a computer installation.

master network processor: a computer programmed to control transmissions on a star network bus, to avoid collisions, to resolve contentions, and to maximize network efficiency.

match: 1: to compare two digital words or bits, looking for equality. 2: to find that equality. 3: to compare the key of a record with another key as a part of a search or selection process.

mathematical simulation: the use of a family of related mathematical equations to produce results representative of a physical system. How well the physical system is simulated depends on its complexity, the requirement for exactness, the mathematical prowess of the constructor, etc. *See* **simulator**.

math menu: in a word processor, the menu of mathematical operations that can be performed on the text.

mathpak: a software package that performs arithmetic computations in a word processing system.

matrix: an orderly rectangular array of elements. The plural is matrices. *See* **dot matrix**.

matrix (word processing): in processing form letters and documents, the main part that stays the same in all versions. There are always two major parts: the matrix (matrix document) and the variables (the parts that change). Within it are markers—control characters that tell the computer where to insert the variables. The matrix is sometimes called the "boiler plate." Synonymous with invoking document. 2: an n-dimensional by m-dimensional rectangular array of numbers that may be added, multipled, or inverted using specified rules of manipulation called matrix algebra. Computers were made for matrix manipulation and vice versa.

matrix document: *See* matrix.

matrix printer: *See* **dot-matrix printer**.

MB or Mbyte: an abbreviation for a megabyte, 1 million 8-bit words.

measure: in typesetting, the width of a line in picas. A pica is $1/6$ of an inch. A 45-pica-wide measure is $7\frac{1}{2}$ inches ($45 \times 1/6$).

mechanical: a camera-ready page, mounted on cardboard, to be placed before the lens and photographed in a photo-offset printing process to produce the negative from which the printing plate will be made.

media-resident software: program instructions and data recorded on some form of changeable medium, such as a floppy disk, magnetic-tape cassette, tape, etc., as opposed to a semiconductor ROM program or some other hard-wired program.

medium: any one of the materials or products used to store word processor or computer programs, documents, and files, such as a floppy disk, tape, cassette, punch card, etc. The plural of medium is media.

mega-:   a prefix from the Greek, meaning 1 million. A megabyte is 1 million bytes; a megahertz is a frequency of 1 million cycles per second.

memory: the part of a computer that receives entered data and stores it for future use. Storage and memory are synonymous. The British prefer to call memory the "store," after a term coined by Babbage, who invented an early but unsuccessful mechanical calculator. Nevertheless, Babbage's machine embodied basic concepts that led to today's digital computers.

memory capacity: the size of the memory in terms of the number of words of data that can be stored there.

memory-management unit or system (MMU): a hardware or software unit associated with larger microcomputers or minicomputers to perform the following functions: dynamically allocate memory as a program runs and tasks are completed; supervise the sharing of common memory areas by different tasks during multitasking without jeopardizing system integrity; detect obvious execution errors related to memory accesses; protect against certain types of memory access; separate user functions from system (or supervisor-state) functions.

memory-mapped display: an implementation of a computer graphics capability that divides the video display screen area into numbered rows and columns of picture elements (pixels). Each pixel has a corresponding memory location in which data that controls it is stored. Rectangular coordinates are used to identify pixel locations. The stored data will determine its color, tint, intensity, etc.

memory plane: in bit-mapped graphics, an area of memory having a 1:1 relationship with the CRT display screen; there may be eight or more memory planes in one graphics system. Each memory location controls the color, tint, intensity, etc., of a corresponding pixel located at one specific point on the screen. Synonymous with bit plane. *See* **bit map**.

memory scrubbing: (slang): *See* **scrog**; **scrub a memory**.

menu: a listing of the options at a given point within a given program.

menu-driven program: 1: a program selected by the operator from a list (menu) of available programs. The desired program is selected by specified keyboard entries, and control is transferred from the menu program to the selected module at run time. 2: a program that offers the user one or more multiple-choice option lists called menus. The menus may be hierarchical in nature, one choice producing another menu for further selection.

merge: to combine elements from two or more similarly ordered sets into one set, arranged in the same order.

message: in data transmission, a serial assemblage of information words in a predetermined format that can be recognized and interpreted by receiving equipment.

MFM: modified-frequency modulation, a technique used in magnetic data recording.

micro-: 1: a prefix from Greek, meaning small, as in microcomputer and microprocessor. 2: a prefix meaning one millionth, as in microampere, micro-volt, and micron (one millionth of a meter).

micro: short for a microcomputer or microprocessor.

microball-point pen: a synonym for a ball-point print head or one of its four ball-point writing instruments.

microcircuit: a synonym for an integrated circuit.

MicroCOBOL: a version of the high-level business-oriented programming language, COBOL, tailored to the constraints of microprocessors.

microcomputer: 1: a small computing machine, typically serving one user at a time, costing less than a few thousand dollars. The distinction between a large microcomputer and a small minicomputer is difficult and unnecessary. It is largely a matter of personal choice. *See* **minicomputer.** 2: a small computer built around an LSI (large-scale integration) microprocessor as its CPU (central processing unit). Early microprocessors needed 4 to 12 additional semiconductor memory and I/O LSI packages to become microcomputers. There are now many single-chip microcomputers on the market. There is nothing small about micro-computer capability; only the size and price tag are small. The minimum microcomputer is a microprocessor CPU plus an operating program in a ROM (read-only memory), a clock oscillator for timing, and a DC power supply.

microelectronic: synonymous with integrated circuit.

microfloppy: a floppy disk measuring 3½ inches in diameter—that's small. Minidisk (diskettes) are 5¼ inches and disks are 8 inches in diameter. But each Sony microfloppy stores 437.5 Kbytes—more than a double-sided, dual-density 5¼-inch diskette.

micrographics: the application of photographic techniques and computers to create tiny, minimum-size copies of documents for storage purposes and automatic information retrieval. Computer Output-On-Microfilm (COM) is one example.

microjustification: the justification of the right margin of a word-processing text by inserting tiny, incremental spaces between letters and words to improve its appearance. In MicroPro's WordStar, this option can be turned off or on; normally, it would be on, but it could throw off the alignment of the columns of a table if it got into the table lines during re-forming or word wrap.

microspacing: synonymous with incremental spacing. Most printers can move only in increments of one character space. (For a 10-pitch font with 10 characters per inch, the minimum space is 1/10 inch.) Some new printers can move 1/10 of a character space (1/100 inch in the above example). Boldfacing is implemented by printing the characters to be emphasized, then backing up to the first character and printing again one incremental space to the right, creating the heavy lines.

microWinchester: a 3.5-inch hard-disk drive, with a thin-film head, plated disk, and negative-pressure air-bearing suspension system, achieving a recording density of 15,000 bits per inch. Control Data Corporation's Cricket 1 has a 5-Mbyte capacity of formatted data, has a 4-by-6.37-inch footprint, and is 1.625 inches high. Standard Winchesters are 14 inches.

middleware: (British): custom system software for a particular user.

milli-:   a prefix from Greek, meaning one thousandth. *Examples:* milliampere, millivolt, millisecond.

milliampere (mA):   a unit of electrical current flow equal to one thousandth of an ampere.

minicomputer: 1: a small digital computer, somewhat larger, usually faster, and more expensive than a microcomputer, but the cost of either is largely a function of its memory size. There is considerable overlap. Wordwise, 16 data bits seems to be the dividing line, but there are machines of that size in both categories, and the Motorola MC68000 microprocessor has 32-bit data word operations. Under 16 bits is definitely micro, but being over 16 bits does not make it a mini. 2: a computer large enough to be used simultaneously by several dozen people working on programs of moderate complexity and size. The cost range is typically $30,000 to $150,000 in 1984 dollars. *See* **microcomputer**.

minidisk, minidiskette: a small floppy disk with a 5.25-inch diameter and a capacity of less than 100K bytes of storage for a single-sided, single-density disk. Double-sided, dual-density disks can store nearly 400,000 formatted bytes of programs or data. An 8-inch disk is a floppy, but the 5.25-inch disk is sometimes called a floppy disk as well.

minifloppy: a small floppy disk. The industry standard minifloppy drive is 5.75 × 3.25 × 8 inches and uses a 5.25-inch minidisk.

misconvergence: the lack of proper convergence of an electron gun beam of electrons in a cathode-ray tube.

MMU: *See* **memory-management unit or system**.

mnemonic: an abbreviation or set of symbols chosen to help the reader remember by association. *Examples:* SUB, a subtract instruction; TZE, transfer on zero accumulator.

mode: one of several ways an equipment or machine can perform. *Example:* a computer and an I/O unit may exchange data in a synchronous or in an asynchronous mode.

modem, MODEM: 1: a modulator/demodulator, an electronic converter required at both ends of a data-transmission link. The modulator puts the information on the carrier during transmission, and the demodulator extracts it from the carrier when receiving. 2: an acoustical coupler, an adapter for transmitting digital data over telephone lines. After the receiving number is dialed, the telephone handset is placed into cushioned muffs on the top of the modem. Serial data inputs are converted into tones that can be sent over the telephone lines. A similar unit on the receiving end changes the tones back into digital data for input to a computer.

modifier: a qualifier add to an instruction to limit, define, or extend its use.

modular: a building-block approach to hardware or software design in which the total system is assembled from functionally organized subassemblies (modules). The modules may or may not be common to other equipment.

modulate: to vary the amplitude, frequency, or phase of a carrier in accordance with an information-carrying signal, usually much lower in amplitude and frequency.

modulation: 1: the act of modulating a carrier with a signal representing information. 2: the signal containing the information.

modulator: 1: a device that modulates a carrier with an information signal. 2: an electronic circuit that produces an alternating current and voltage proportional to a direct-current (DC) input.

module: 1: a component of a hardware or software system that is designed to be easily removed for repair or replacement with a minimum effect on the rest of the system. 2: a package constructed using a modular approach to design. *See* **modular.**

monitor: 1: to watch over for a period of time. 2: *See* **monitor program.** 3: short for video monitor, a TV video-display device used to observe what is happening in front of the camera. 4: any device that monitors. ***Example:*** a voltage-monitor circuit that puts out a failure signal when a supply goes outside its acceptable range of operating voltage limits.

monitor program: the firmware nonvolatile program (in ROM) that must be resident in every computer when the power is first applied. It gets its name because it monitors the keyboard or front-panel switches, looking for operator inputs. Most microcomputer monitors include a restart/initialize routine on power-up, keyboard scan and decode, plus some program development and troubleshooting commands such as memory examine/change, register display/change, punch and load tape, etc. Monitors are for the small computer without disk-drive capability.

monochrome: pertaining to a single-color CRT or video terminal screen. The most popular screen colors are amber, green, and white. Not color.

monospace type: a type size and style adhering strictly to the uniform pitch (characters per inch) and not employing microspacing or proportional spacing for a more pleasing appearance.

most significant byte (MSB):   the byte having the greatest effect on the value of a multiple-byte quantity.

motherboard: an interconnecting assembly into which printed-circuit cards or boards or modules are connected. The cards, boards, or modules are daughters.

mouse: a small box with wheels and a 24-inch wire tail that plugs into an input port on your computer. A mouse is a CRT cursor-mover. When rolled around on a desk top, it sends an electronic signal back through the tail to move the cursor in the same direction and in proportion to the amount of movement. On the top of the mouse, one or more push-button switches are located; they allow you to transfer items moved by the mouse from one window to the next, edit text, select from a menu, or whatever your software allows. Mice are one of the features of Apple's Lisa computer, but over 60 personal and business computer manufacturers are evaluating their use. People who are not trained typists find the mouse particularly useful.

multi-:   1: a prefix meaning many. 2: short for a multivibrator.

multidrop link: in local area networks (LANs) a single line shared by two or more nodes. Synonymous with multipoint link. *See* **node**.

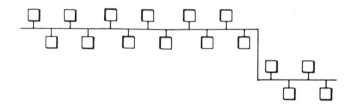

multifont: describing a print head having more than one character set, usually with a different typeface, such as italics or Greek alphabet. Such a head is most useful when one typeface, such as italics, is embedded in a page of ordinary text.

multifunction system: a word-processing system that can execute a broad spectrum of related ancillary tasks, such as mathematical operations on data and communications between stations, as opposed to one that cannot.

multiple-column sort: a sort operation on a data file involving more than one column.

multiple-line sort: a sort operation on a data file that consists of multiple-line blocks of information, such as a mailing list, where each block of data to be sorted consists of a name, street address, city, zip code, telephone number, etc.

multiple viewports: in computer graphics, several CRT displays that show different portions of a display whose "world" coordinates are too large to display on a single CRT screen of "local" coordinates. *See* **viewport; window; world coordinates.**

multiple workstation system: a word-processing or office automation system with two or more input terminals (workstations).

multiplex: to cause two or more signals to share the use of a channel or wire. Time multiplexing and frequency multiplexing are the two most widely used techniques.

multiplexer: a device that multiplexes two or more signals for transmission on a single channel. Also spelled multiplexor.

multipoint link: a synonym for a multidrop link.

multiprocessing: 1: two or more processors connected to a common system bus performing in a computing network. One processor at a time acts as controller, and the others are slaves. Each may have access to the others' memories; they may share a common memory and other resources, such as a printer and a tape transport. 2: the simultaneous execution of two or more computer programs by a computer network.

multiprocessor: a processor sharing the same bus system and often the same resources, such as memory and peripheral units, with several other processors, decentralizing computing power within a given system. A processor that is part of a multiprocessing system. A protocol must be established, with one computer at a time acting as a controller and the rest acting as slaves.

multiprogramming: 1: a capability of some computer operating systems and hardware to run several programs concurrently; each is called a process, with its own set of system resources. 2: the overlapping or interleaving of the executions of several programs by some operating systems.

multirunning: (British): multiprogramming.

multistation: describing a communications network with two or more data terminals.

multistrike: an advanced printer capability of striking a selected character two or three times during printout to create a boldface, emphasized character.

multitasking: a computer system operating environment in which each "process" can perform several different tasks at the same time. Each task can respond individually to the requirements of its own environment. *See* **process.**

MUX: a common abbreviation for a multiplexer, a device that multiplexes (causes two or more signals to share the use of a channel or wire).

mW: milliwatt, one thousandth of a watt, a unit of electrical power.

N

NAK: the negative acknowledgment signal in teletypewriter communications, a signal sent by the receiver to the sender as a negative response to indicate that the previous transmission was unacceptable.

narrow measure: in typesetting, the width of a column of type filling somewhat less than half the page width. *Example:* a measure of 14 picas ($14 \times \frac{1}{6}$ inch $= 2\frac{1}{3}$ inches) is narrow. A typical book-size page is 24 picas.

national character set: the alphabet of a foreign language or ethnic group, such as Greek, Chinese, Arabic, or Russian.

nested loop: a program loop that lies within another loop. In the following BASIC code, loop B is nested within loop A:

```
10 FOR I = 1 TO 3; This is loop A
20     PRINT I,
30     FOR J = 1 TO 10; This is loop B
40         PRINT J;
50     NEXT J; This is the end of loop B
60 NEXT I; This is the end of loop A
```

Loop B will be executed 10 times each time that loop A is executed, for a total of 30 times.

nested subroutine: a subroutine called from another subroutine and executed as a part of the execution of the first subroutine. *See* **nesting**.

nesting: placing one loop or subroutine within another, structurally the same as nested boxes or tables.

nesting level: in nested FOR-NEXT loops or subroutines, the outermost loop is the first nesting level. Each time a loop is placed within another loop, the nesting level increases. Nesting levels greater than three or four are unusual.

network: the interconnection of several terminals and/or computers to share common facilities, such as data banks, peripherals, etc. If the facilities are in the same building, the connection is usually by a shielded coaxial cable and a serial transmission protocol, such as the EIA's RS-232C format. When the separation is between buildings separated by more than a few yards, telephone lines and modems are normally required.

network topology: the geometric arrangement of the links and nodes that make up a network. *Example:* the star configuration with a central processor at the center and each station on the end of a radial arm.

nexus: a point at which connections occur in a circuit or system. A rarely used synonym for a node.

nil pointer: the pointer to the end of a chained list.

N-key rollover: a feature of some keyboards; each key does not have to be released before the next key is pressed. Ordinary keys do.

node: in local area network topology, an end point to any branch of a network or a junction common to two or more branches.

no-file menu: in MicroPro's WordStar word-processing program, a preliminary menu that appears right after the copyright credits, version number, serial number, etc., but before you've had a chance to specify a file to work on.

nonbreak space: a space that occurs within, and is part of, a name of somebody or something. *Example:* J. P. Brown II looks strange as J. P. Brown II. There are two kinds of spaces between words: regular spaces that should fall at the end of a line, if possible, and nonbreak spaces that should be avoided at the end of a line.

nonimpact printer: a printer using a print head that does not function by impact. *Examples:* ink-jet, thermal, and electrosensitive printers. *See* **impact printer.**

noninterlaced scanning: *See* **interlace.**

nonnumeric: 1: referring to any alphabetic character, punctuation mark, or other symbol, except the decimal digits 0–9. 2: describing an operation that does not involve numeric characters or operations.

non-return-to-zero format (NRZ): in digital data transmission, a serial binary data format in which the signal or recording voltage does not return to the zero level for each 1 bit, but changes only for a 1-to-0 or a 0-to-1 transition. *See* **return-to-zero format**.

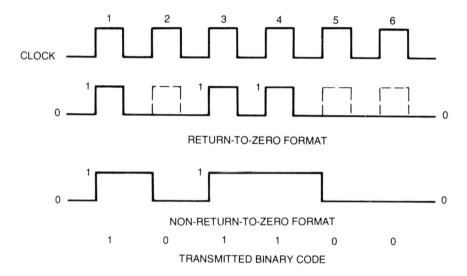

North American Presentation Level Protocol System (NAPLPS): an AT&T graphics communications protocol based on the Canadian Teledon system for the transmission of graphics and text over standard communications systems.

notch: the write-protect notch, the largest notch on the bottom of a disk or diskette. With 8-inch floppies, an adhesive tab must be affixed to enable recording (writing). With the 5¼-inch minidisks, the exact opposite is true; the tab must be removed for writing.

notebook computer: a small portable computer, such as Epson's HX-20, Hewlett-Packard's HP75, and Radio Shack's Model 100. Notebook computers fit inside a briefcase. Principal applications: calendar and scheduling, rolodex address/telephone data storage and retrieval, front-end word processing, numerical calculations, etc.

numeric: one of the decimal digits from 0 to 9, sometimes with an associated plus or minus sign, as opposed to an alphabetic character or punctuation symbol.

numerical analysis: the quantitative study of or solutions to a problem defined by mathematical expressions. It may also include a study of the errors and error limits involved in the choice of solution.

numerical control: the automatic control of a machine using numerical input data, generally introduced while the operation is in process. Numerical control is digital, incremental, or discrete, as opposed to continuous, analog, or proportional control.

numerical keyboard: synonymous with numerical keypad.

numerical keypad: a small calculator keyboard arranged with the same key layout as an accounting calculator to facilitate the high-speed entry of numerical data.

numeric code: a code set that represents only numbers and their associated characters, but not alphabetics, as opposed to an alphanumeric code that can express either numbers or alphabet characters.

numeric sort: a sort that arranges a list in ascending or descending numerical order, as opposed to an alphabetic sort.

object computer: synonymous with target computer or target processor, the more popular term at the moment.

object deck or pack: an obsolescent term for the group or set of punched cards that contain the object-program output of a card punch.

object language: a fully compiled or assembled program in executable machine code ready for loading into a computer. An object program is the output of a source-program input to an assembler or compiler. *See* **object deck or pack**; **object program**.

object module: synonymous with object program.

object pack: *See* **object deck or pack**.

object program: the output of a source-program input to an assembler or a compiler. With the older card punch/card reader I/O, it was an object deck of cards. Today, it is just a separate disk file of executable binary machine code.

object routine: synonymous with object program.

OCR: *See* **optical character recognition**.

OCR character: a printable character having a specified size, shape, and form readable by automatic optical-character-recognition equipment.

OCR wand: an OCR hand-held device that converts the familiar supermarket bar codes (or other OCR codes) into microprocessor-compatible digital outputs. One manufacturer's model can read all common bar-code formats printed with a minimum bar width of 0.3 mm by focusing light from an internal LED emitting at 700 nm and sensing the reflected light with an integrated silicon photodetector. TTL- and CMOS-compatible outputs are produced by signal-conditioning circuits.

octal: 1: pertaining to the number 8 or consisting of eight unique parts. 2: short for the octal number system with 8 as its base or radix.

octal code: data expressed in the octal number system. Usually, octal code is used as a shorthand way of writing binary numbers for legibility and error detection and prevention.

octal number system: the number system with 8 as its base or radix. Its symbols are 0, 1, 2, 3, 4, 5, 6, and 7 only. Counting in octal is as easy as counting in decimal: 0, 1, 2, 3, 4, 5, 6, 7 . . . 10, 11, 12, 13, 14, 15, 16, 17 . . . 20, 21, 22, 23, 24, 25, 26, 27 . . . 30, 31, etc. An octal number has an octal point.

$$
\begin{array}{ccccccccc}
& 512 & 64 & 8 & 1 & . & 1/8 & 1/64 & 1/512 \\
\text{Weight} & 8^3 & 8^2 & 8^1 & 8^0 & . & 8^{-1} & 8^{-2} & 8^{-3} \\
& 1 & 1 & 5 & 2 & . & 0 & 0 & 0
\end{array}
$$

$$(1\ 1\ 5\ 2\ .\ 0)_8 = 1 \times 512 + 1 \times 64 + 5 \times 8 + 2 \times 1 = (6\ 1\ 8)_{10}$$

octal point: the radix point in the octal number system; the digits to the left of the octal point represent positive powers of the base 8, and the digits to the right of the octal point represent negative powers of 8.

off-line: describing a device or operation not under the control of a central processing unit and usually not connected to its I/O bus. *Example:* a card-punch machine used to prepare punch cards, while the computer is doing other things. The opposite is on-line.

off-line mode: synonymous with off-line.

OMNInet: a local area network for tying personal computers into an integrated system. OMNInet is a trademark of Corvus Systems.

on-line: describing an operation performed on or by a peripheral unit connected to the I/O bus of a digital computer and controlled by it. Most computer I/O involves on-line operations with devices such as printers, modems, magnetic-tape drives, floppy-disk drives, etc.

open: to enable a computer file for reading or writing. A file must be created before it can be opened, and it must be opened before it can be used for either reading or writing. In a multiuser system, who can read or write to a file is determined by its access control list or its file attributes; both are defined by the owner of the file.

open a file: to prepare a disk file for reading or writing. The computer's operating system does this through an interpreter, compiler, data-base manager, etc. Most extended BASICs with file-handling capabilities have an OPEN FILE command.

open a window: In integrated software systems, such as Apple Computer's Lisa and VisiCorp's Visi On™, to display the contents of a file in a window on the CRT screen. *See* **window.** The window is opened when the file is "grabbed." *See* **grab a file.** Three or more windows may be open at any time.

open quote: in printing and typing, the starting quotation mark at the beginning or left end of the expression. The right mark is a close quote.

operating system: 1: the group of software and/or firmware programs that bring a computer to life, give it its capability, and implement its many functions. It may have any or all of the following programs: bootstrap loader, I/O drivers, assembler, compiler, linker/loader, queue handler, task scheduler, editor/debugger, interpreter, interrupt handler, data-base manager, librarian. *See* **disk operating system.** 2: pertaining to a computer that is up and running.

operating system monitor: one of the utility programs of the operating system. Its primary function is the monitoring of front-panel switches and the processing of their inputs.

operation: 1: a defined action; namely, the act of obtaining a result from one or more operands in accordance with a rule that completely specifies the result for a permissible combination of operands. 2: the set of such acts specified by such a rule, or the rule itself. 3: the act specified by a single computer instruction. 4: a program step undertaken or executed by a computer. *Examples:* addition, comparison, shifting, transfer, etc. The operation is usually specified by the operation-code field of the instruction. 5: the event or specific action performed by a logic element.

operator: the mathematical or logic symbols that represent a required operation between two or more variables or constants. *Examples:* $+$, $-$, $\cdot$, $/$.

optical character recognition (OCR):   the automatic reading of special alphanumeric type fonts by electro-optical equipment that can scan across a line of printed characters and convert each one into a binary code understandable to a computer. The optical sensors may be fixed with the material to be read moving, or a movable hand-held OCR wand may be passed over the characters to be input.

optical disk: a synonym for a video disk or videodisc, an aluminum platter about the size of a 33¹/₃-rpm audio record, but used with an optical drive to store up to 4 billion characters of read-only computer data. That is 40 times what a typical 7-inch reel of magnetic tape can hold and 1.5 times the amount you can store on an entire magnetic-disk drive. One square inch of its surface can hold 25 copies of *Gone with the Wind*. It is an emerging technology. Optical disks cannot be erased. The data are recorded with a laser that melts tiny pits in the aluminum surface. Another laser reads the data by sensing changes in reflectivity between the pitted (digital 1s) and nonpitted (digital 0s) surfaces.

optical drive: an electromechanical system including the drive and electronics for optical disks.

optical memory: a storage technology based on video-disk technology. *See* **optical-storage subsystem.**

optical-storage subsystem: a developing secondary-storage technology consisting of one or more optical disks in a compatible drive mechanism. Each aluminum disk spins at 1300 rpm in the drive made by Storage Technology Corporation. Present disks are read-only and incapable of erasure. Erasable versions are in development. Systems are priced over $100,000 now, but this technology may be the wave of the future. The Japanese and others are working on competitive versions and prices are bound to come down with time. *See* **optical disk.**

optimization: the technique of studying or changing the parameters of a process, control system, logic design, computer program, etc., in an attempt to achieve the best possible performance in terms of high speed, minimum cost, minimum memory requirements, or some compromise combination of design parameters.

order: 1: a class of things grouped according to value or quantity. 2: describing the relative value of a computer byte or word with respect to another. *Example:* the higher-order byte in a word is the more significant byte. 3: to arrange a group of items according to any specified rule or set of rules. 4: the arrangement of a group of items according to one or more rules. 5: synonymous with sort. 6: synonymous with instruction.

order of magnitude: a range of magnitude extending from some value to 10 times that value. Usually, the reference is to the exponent of the base 10 when a number is expressed in scientific notation as a coefficient multiplied by 10 raised to some power.

originate/answer modem: a modem that sends (originates) or receives (answers) data over phone lines, depending on the position of a manual switch. Some modems automatically dial (autodial) a destination number if the associated computer is programmed for it.

OS: *See* **operating system.**

output: information transmitted by the computer to an external device.

output driver program: a time-share service term used to describe a program used by the customer to retrieve and list a "background" program entered earlier using an input driver program.

output limited: the usual case for modern processors in which processing speed is limited by the slower I/O units, not the inherent greater speed of the central processor.

output queue: a buffer-storage area for messages produced by a computer and placed in a queue, waiting for delayed transmission to external devices.

output routine: a software subprogram that executes some or all of the necessary functions involved in the output of computer data to one or more peripheral devices.

overhead: that portion of a software routine or procedure that is necessary to get things ready or to put them away, but that is not really a part of the processing. Sometimes overhead is called housekeeping.

overlay: a memory-management technique that reuses the same area of read/write memory at different times during a program run. When a routine has been executed and is no longer needed, it is overwritten in part or in entirety by a replacement routine to be run later.

overlay (graphics): an alphanumeric message or a symbol that should remain stationary on a moving background on a CRT screen display. Overlays are implemented with an additional memory plane in bit-mapped graphics.

P

package: 1: an integrated circuit in its plastic or ceramic housing. 2: a software program or set of programs sold to the general public. 3: in structured analysis, to transform logic functions into modules, programs, and job steps, identifying and defining distinct physical units for machine execution.

packet: 1: a number of letters sent at one time. 2: a small group or mass. 3: in data communications, a small number of blocks transmitted at the same time, in burst mode.

packet switching: the transmission of messages in packets from node to node in a network, usually in burst mode, to keep the channel quiet most of the time.

packing density: the number of bits recorded per unit length on a magnetic tape or on one track of a disk, diskette, or minidisk; 1600 bits per inch (bpi) is common using phase encoding, 6400 bpi is often seen, and even higher packing is possible using special equipment.

pad: 1: short for keypad. 2: to use a dummy character, word, or record to fill out a predetermined format of fixed size.

pad character: a character used to pad a word, block, or record to a predetermined size.

padding: a term borrowed from journalism to describe the addition of dummy words, characters, records, etc., to a block of stored information to reach a predetermined size for ease of handling or for some other reason. Zeros are usually added for padding.

page, paging: 1: the basic unit of relocation and protection in a virtual-address memory space. 2: a memory-management system partition of the user address space into fixed-size divisions. Two differences delineate paging from segmentation: (1) segments have variable lengths, but pages are fixed in size; (2) in a paged memory, a task accesses memory using a single address, not a segment register number plus an added address displacement.

page address: the field of the total address (virtual or physical) that defines the page containing the desired address in a paged memory system.

page composition: *See* **makeup**.

page length: the length of text from the top edge of the first line of characters to the bottom edge of the last line of characters. Fifty-four lines of text make a 9-inch page with 1 inch margins at the top and bottom on a standard 8½-by-11-inch sheet of paper.

page offset: the number of columns a word-processing text is moved over from the left side of the printer, in addition to the left margin and any other spaces and indentations in the file. Page offset allows additional room for punching and binding a text.

pagination: in computers, the arrangement and number of pages in memory, if the memory is paged; in publishing, the act of numbering the pages in a book.

paging: *See* **page**.

painting: in computer color graphics, filling in a closed shape or area with a solid color, tint, crosshatch, etc.

palette: the total number of colors and tints (shades of color) that a given computer graphics system can display. For a high-resolution bit-mapped system with eight memory planes, over 16,000,000 different values can be displayed, but only 256 can be used at any one time.

pan: in computer graphics, to simulate on the CRT screen the effect of a rotating motion-picture or television camera, keeping an object in view, or to achieve a panoramic effect on the video terminal screen.

paper burster: an office machine that separates continuous forms by tearing them at the perforations between individual sheets. Some are electric; some manual.

paper tape: a nearly obsolete method of storing computer data by punching or perforating coded holes across a 1-inch-wide strip of paper. Some hobbyists on limited budgets still use paper tape. *See* **punch tape**.

paper-tape reader: a nearly obsolete device that senses the patterns of punched or perforated holes in paper or Mylar tape and translates them into electrical signals for input into a digital computer. The tape is usually wound on 5- to 7-inch reels and pulled past an optical or mechanical sensor that converts the coded holes into corresponding binary codes for input to the computer.

paper throw: a paper advance in a printer caused by a line-feed or form-feed character, not merely to the next character position.

parser: the first or second pass of a compiler program that analyzes a program syntactically and passes flow graphs and parse trees to the code generator.

passive: having no transistors or other active devices that provide power amplification and gain to compensate for internal losses. Not active.

password: in time-sharing and multiuser environments, a unique set of digits or alphanumeric characters assigned to each user; only the user and his authorized representatives know the password. It must be typed in when prompted by the operating system before access can be made to the user's files. Password protection may also be assigned to individual files, but usually they are secured with file attributes or access control lists.

paste-up: a synonym for a makeup or page composition. *See* **makeup**.

patch: 1: to modify a computer program in a small and usually expedient way, generally employing manual coding and keyboard entry.

path: one of the many routes through a sequence of instructions that contain branch, jump, or transfer instructions.

pathname: a prefix symbol added to a file name to describe the route to take from the user's directory to some other directory to get to a desired file (some operating systems).

pattern: a string used to scan another string to determine if the first string is a substring of the second.

pattern recognition: 1: the identification of shapes, forms, colors, contrasts, configurations, etc., by automatic means, usually involving a video camera and optical scanner. 2: the recognition of electrical voltages or other signals to extract information. *Example:* a voice pattern.

PC board (PCB): short for printed-circuit board. Synonymous with PC card.

PCM: pulse code modulation, a technique used in digital data transmission in which the frequency or amplitude of a carrier is modulated with information in some prearranged digital code.

p-code: short for pseudocode. *See* **pseudomachine.**

pel: (British): short for a pixel, an elemental area of a video terminal screen, the smallest individually addressable area.

pen graphics: a feature of some plotters with ink pen writing styli, usually in colors. Under computer control, the pens can be made to draw lines, arcs, areas, polygons, and other graphic designs.

perforated tape: synonymous with punch tape, a generic term for paper or Mylar.

peripheral: 1: an I/O device controlled by a computer but not considered part of it. *Example:* a printer or floppy disk. 2: pertaining to such an on-line or off-line device. 3: short for a peripheral unit.

peripheral-limited: synonymous with I/O limited; a computer system in which the throughput is limited by the slower I/O units, not the processor. This is generally the case.

peripheral unit: *See* **peripheral.**

permanent memory: stored data that remains unchanged when power is interrupted or removed. Nonvolatile means the same thing.

persistence of vision: the ability of the human eye and brain to retain an image for an appreciable time after the removal of the stimulus that created it. Persistence of vision makes movies and TV possible.

personal computer: a computer designed for the exclusive use by a single user, or at least one user at a time. Personal computers range from hobby units costing less than $100 to sophisticated scientific machines at $50,000 and up. One MIT system, called the V, uses a 64-bit-wide multiplexed bus with 32 address bits and 32 data bits. It will handle up to 20 megabytes of disk storage and up to 8 megabytes of 64K MOS RAM main memory, plus much much more.

personality module: an adapter, usually a plug-in, that mechanically and electrically allows a universal test, development, or PROM programmer system to operate with a specific microelectronic device. *Example:* a PROM programmer will have a personality module for each of the different types of PROMs that the equipment is designed to program.

PERT: an acronym for Program Evaluation and Review Technique, a critical-path project/program planning method invented in Robert McNamara's days as secretary of defense and still used today. It is computer-compatible, and what's more, it works.

phantom rubout: a special character of fully formed character printers (they have thimbles or daisy-wheel print heads); it varies depending on the daisy wheel or thimble used. Usually, it is a double underline or a graphic symbol.

phantom space: a special character of fully formed character printers, such as a thimble or daisy wheel. The symbol depends on the particular printer; usually it is a cent sign, ¢, or the pound sign, #.

phase encoding: a self-clocking binary code in which the information is in the direction of the phase (polarity) change that occurs in the middle of each bit time. *Examples:* the Manchester codes. *See* **Manchester code.**

philoxenic: (British): the British answer to "user-friendly."

phoneme: any one of the primitive units of speech in which the sounds of words, phrases, and sentences in a given language can be analyzed.

phosphor: a substance that exhibits luminescence when struck by high-energy particles, such as the electrons from an electron gun in a cathode-ray tube. The inside of the front face of the tube is coated with a phosphor.

phosphor dots: the blue, green, and red circular elements on the inside of a color TV or monitor tube. They luminesce when struck by accelerated electrons from the appropriate electron gun to form the color image on the tube.

phosphorescence: the physical property of a substance to emit light for a relatively long period (persistence) after the energy source has been removed; a basic principle of cathode-ray and television tubes.

photocomposition: a synonym for phototypesetting, a process that employs photographic means to create a relief printing surface. *See* **phototypesetter.**

phototypesetter: a machine used to produce ("set") publication-quality printed documents, having virtually replaced the "hot-lead" types. The machine uses a lens system and light-sensitive paper similar to photographic print paper. Type fonts are disks or drums of opaque glass, plastic, or film with transparent characters concentrically arranged around the perimeter. A beam of light passes through the selected character, through a magnifying lens and fiber optics, to shine on the paper. The exposed paper is then developed in a chemical bath. Black characters emerge where the light reached the paper. Photo-composers typically have four to eight different type styles on each changeable type font, ranging from 5½ points to 72 points in size (one point = 1/72 inch). Synonymous with photocomposer.

physical record: the smallest unit of data an I/O peripheral device can transfer. *Example:* 80 characters on an 80-column punched card. The card reader's physical record is 80 bytes.

PI: programmed instruction. The material to be learned is presented in short sequential fragments called frames. Each frame explains a concept or presents a set of related facts to be learned and ends with a test, usually multiple choice. Correct answers lead to the next frame in the standard sequence; incorrect answers lead to one or more remedial learning paths. PI has existed in book form for many years. Computer-aided instruction (CAI) is often nothing more than PI on the CRT. PI as a sequence of frames without branches is called linear PI; with branching it is called branched or branching PI.

pica: 1: a unit of length in typesetting; there are six picas per inch. Each pica is 12 points (72 points per inch). 2: a common type font that prints at 10 pitch (10 characters per inch).

pie chart: a common graphics figure used to show the percentage breakdown of a whole into its component parts as pie-shaped sections of a circle.

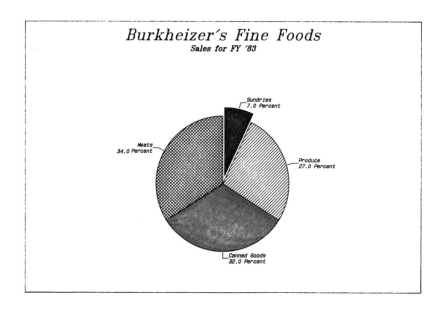

pin feed: a commonly used technique and implementation to align and feed a continuous roll of printer paper by means of sprocket wheels at both edges of the form. Pins located around the circumference of the sprocket wheels engage uniformly spaced guide holes in the paper. Synonymous with sprocket feed and tractor feed.

pin feeder: a common mechanization for paper advance in automatic printers. Pins located in sprockets along both ends of the platen engage holes on each edge of the paper to control its movement. Synonymous with sprocket feeder and tractor feeder.

pin-feed paper: fanfold or business-form paper with sprocket holes for paper feed on both sides.

pitch: the number of characters per inch in a printed text; common typewriter values are 8, 10, and 12 pitch. Typesetters use a completely different type-sizing system: 72 points = one inch. Type size is measured in points, not pitch.

pixel: a unit picture element in solid-state imaging chips for video cameras. A TI CCD chip measuring 700 mils on a side is 800×800 pixels or 640,000 picture elements.

pixel plane: a synonym for a bit plane, memory plane, visual plane, and video plane in bit-mapped computer graphics. The marketers are restless tonight.

pixel rate: a figure of merit for graphics memory access speeds. The value for one Texas Instruments DRAM (dynamic random-access memory) is 125 MHz.

platen: the backing, usually a cylindrical roller of hard rubber or similar material, placed behind the paper in an impact printer. Each key strikes the paper, resting firmly against the platen.

playback head: the read head in magnetic-tape units that have separate read and write heads.

playout: the printing out or typing out of a word-processor document.

plotter: a computer-controlled graphics equipment that uses ink or thermal pens to produce lines, curves, arcs, etc., by moving the pen along the paper (or the paper with respect to the pen). Plotters are devices that use line segments to create figures. They can plot in colors with more than one pen and ink supply.

p-machine: short for pseudomachine. *See* **pseudomachine.**

point: a typesetting unit of length equal to 1/72 inch (1 inch = 72 points); 12 points = 1 pica.

point size: the height of a character measured in points. *See* **point.** Typical character heights range from 4.5 to 72 points. Don't scale the height of the character to determine its point size; the length of ascenders and descenders are part of the point size, as well as a small amount of space above and below the letter. Books are usually set in 9, 10, or 11 point.

6 point

9 point

10 point

12 point

14 point

24 point

point-to-point link: in local area network topology, a circuit that connects two, and only two, nodes without passing through an intermediate node.

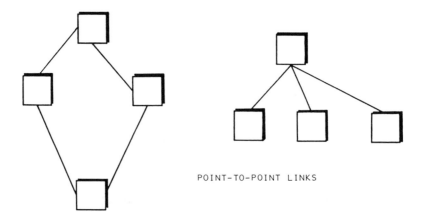

POINT-TO-POINT LINKS

polarized plug: a plug designed to be inserted into its mating socket in only one unique orientation to prevent misconnection of circuits.

polarizing slot: a slot cut into the edge of a printed-circuit card to prevent the insertion of the card into the wrong card-edge connector or upside down. The polarizing slots are associated with mating bars or other mechanical hindrances to insertion.

poll: to perform the polling operation.

polygon: in computer graphics, a generic term for a many-sided, closed figure; the perimeter is usually straight-line segments.

polygon fill: in graphics, the painting of a closed area with a uniform solid tint, crosshatch, etc. Polygon fill is a general term for area fills that include rectangles, squares, etc. The required time is a measure of graphics processing speed.

port: 1: short for I/O port. 2: one or more terminals that provide electrical input and/or output to a circuit or system. A port may be a single line for serial I/O or a bus system of several lines for parallel I/O, one line for each bit of the data word.

portability of software: that attribute of a computer program that allows it to run on more than one computer (the more the better). Portability is achieved by writing the program in a standard common high-level language, such as BASIC, without extensions.

port terminator: a dummy connector used to load (terminate) properly a computer system bus under certain conditions. *Example:* when using a Radio Shack Model II computer built-in disk drive, you must plug a port terminator into the port connector to the expansion stand-alone disk-drive system.

power-fail interrupt/auto-restart: a feature of some minicomputers and microcomputers. When power fails, an automatic hardware interrupt is generated by the falling line voltage, causing the CPU to branch to a power-fail routine in ROM. When power is restored, the interrupted program resumes without error.

A few milliseconds are available before the 60-hertz power-line voltage falls to levels that affect the DC low-voltage power supplies. During this period, hundreds of instructions can be executed to prepare the computer for the loss of power, preventing loss or alteration of data.

precision: the degree of exactness of a specified quantity. In a digital value, precision is determined by the resolution, the number of bits used to express the quantity. *Example:* if the degrees in a circle are represented by an 8-bit byte that can have 256 different discrete values, the precision is 360/256 or a little more than 1.4 degrees. Precision should not be confused with accuracy, which is related to the number of errors in the data. A three-place sine table without errors is more accurate than a seven-place table with five errors, but it is certainly less precise.

preprocess: to perform preliminary operations on data, usually at the time and point of generation, before transmitting the data to a computer for further processing.

preprocessor: a software program that translates one set of symbols into another. *Example:* a SMAL-80 macropreprocessor converts the complete set of ASCII characters and control codes into corresponding assembly-language mnemonics that an assembler can recognize and translate into machine code.

primary sort: the first sort in a multiple-variable list or file. *Example:* to sort the names of New Yorkers from a national director of names is a primary sort. If the people living on Long Island are sorted from the list of New Yorkers, this operation is a secondary sort.

primitive: not derivative, but primary, elemental, or basic. A primitive form is a basic building block from which other forms are derived; synonymous with root.

printed-circuit (PC) card or board: an epoxy or other plastic board on which electronic components (resistors, capacitors, integrated circuits, diodes, transistors, transformers, etc.) are mounted and interconnected by plated or etched foil conducting paths.

printed-wiring board (PWB):   synonymous with printed-circuit card or board.

printer: a typewriterlike computer peripheral that produces a hard-copy paper printout of computer data under the control of a central processor. There are all kinds: high-speed, line, character, impact, daisy-wheel, thermal, etc.

printer buffer: an electronics interface assembly used between a computer and its printer. The computer outputs text to the buffer and then is available for other tasks; the buffer is usually a smart device, a dedicated microprocessor to control the printer, freeing the main computer for better things while the printing is being done.

printer selector DIP switch: a DIP switch used to select one particular printer in a system where more than one is available.

printer spooler: a disk area reserved for buffer storage of printing jobs that are queued up, awaiting printer availability.

printer terminal: a computer I/O unit with a keyboard for input and a printer for hard-copy output. They are widely used by time-share services, such as General Electric, which connect hundreds or thousands of users to a large mainframe through the use of acoustic couplers, modems, and telephone lines. In this application, hard-copy printouts are highly desirable, often mandatory.

print head: the part of a printer mechanism that puts the character on the paper.

print-head slew rate: the rotational speed at which a circular print head, such as a daisy wheel or thimble, can advance a new character into printing position.

printout: 1: the hard-copy print of computer data by a printer under CPU control. 2: to output computer data to a printer.

print wheel: the element containing the type font in an automatic printer or typewriter.

priority: the order of importance assigned to processes or pending actions.

procedure: 1: a step-by-step definition of one way to solve a problem. 2: a structured programming term that describes that part of a subprogram exclusive of the header, data type declarations, and other nonexecutable parts. 3: a subprogram or routine, a separate part of a program that can be called into execution by its name.

process: 1: to perform a systematic series of actions directed to an end result. 2: the systematic procedure. 3: in a multitasking environment on a minicomputer or one of the 16-bit microcomputers, one of the tasks being executed. 4: in multiprogramming, the set of system resources (files, memory space, etc.) allocated to a particular user. Each user's process is like a complete computer system, with its memory allocation and its own distinct programming console, and it has access to all of the system peripherals (printers, disk files, magnetic-tape transports, etc.).

processor: 1: a device that processes. 2: short for microprocessor. 3: a software program that includes the compiling, translating, and other functions of a given programming language, such as a BASIC processor or COBOL processor.

processor-limited: the unusual case in data processing in which the throughput of a computer system is limited by the speed of the central processor, not by the slower peripheral units.

processor-time efficiency: in a time-sharing multiuser system, the percentage of the total time of operation that the system is actually running user programs. Total time includes user-program execution time plus the overhead or housekeeping time required to manage the system and change users.

profile: the file of data that must be entered by a user of a time-share computer during the login process. The computer uses the data to identify the user, limit his resources, and store his password.

program: 1: a series of actions scheduled to achieve a given result. 2: a list of sequential instructions or statements written to produce a specified result by a computer. 3: to design, write, or test such a list of instructions. 4: an abstract statement of an algorithm and a description of the data to be processed by that algorithm.

program language: a vocabulary of terms and the set of conventions for connecting these terms together for the purpose of communicating one's thoughts to a computer and to other persons.

program library: a collection of available computer programs, procedures, and routines, usually tested, debugged, and of general use and applicability. More likely than not, the library is physically one or more magnetic disks or tapes.

program linking: the joining together of separate programs or parts of programs, usually by a software utility called a linking loader or a linker-loader program.

program listing: a sequential numerical list of the instructions or statements that constitute a program. Usually, a program list is prepared manually, whereas a program listing is the computer-controlled output list to a CRT video terminal or a hard-copy printer.

programmable: capable of being programmed, as a programmable calculator, which can sequence itself automatically through a series of operations under the direction of an internal program. In the microcomputer world, it means user-programmable, such as a PROM (a programmable read-only memory) or EPROM (erasable programmable read-only memory), as opposed to a ROM (read-only memory), which is programmable only at the factory during fabrication.

program maintenance: the process of keeping a program free of bugs and current by updating it as required. Synonymous with software maintenance. Maintenance costs are usually several times the initial acquisition cost of the program.

programme: (British): an optional spelling for program.

programmed halt: a halt instruction written into a program to stop the computer run for some purpose, such as entry of data, examination of register contents, etc. Synonymous with coded stop.

programmer: 1: ideally, a person who thinks out a logical solution to a problem, implementing it with a detailed plan and translating it into a written language that a computer can understand and convert into an executable machine code. Sometimes, however, the programmer is merely a coder who encodes the flowcharts or other diagrams and verbal instructions of a systems analyst. 2: an electromechanical device that executes a preset sequence of actions. *Example:* in an automatic washer.

programmer/analyst: a programmer who performs the work and responsibilities of a system analyst.

program tape: a paper or magnetic tape on which a computer program has been stored for later use, providing an automatic way of entering it into the computer. Program tape is, in general, a backup storage method, and paper tape is nearly obsolete, except for hobbyists.

prompt: 1: a symbol on a CRT screen or printer, generated by a computer program, indicating that it is ready to accept commands. For example, in some BASICs the computer prints an asterisk (*) when ready for a new program statement or keyboard command. Others may use the right parenthesis,), for the same purpose.

proof: 1: a preliminary copy for proofreading. 2: to proofread.

proofread: to read a text looking for errors: typos, spelling, capitalization, paragraphing, and everything else.

proportional joystick: a joystick with linear DC outputs, as opposed to ON–OFF types (0 volts ON or +5 VDC OFF, for example).

proportional spacing: a technique used by some word processors and printers to right-justify a printed line. The space between characters is not uniform, but it is proportionally increased or decreased to make every line length come out the same, regardless of the number or type of characters.

protocol: a term borrowed from the diplomatic world and applied to rules for communication between different computers or computer peripherals over a common bus system. The bus protocol is a formal definition that defines how data must be formatted, what handshaking (control) signals must be exchanged and when, order and priority of various messages, etc., etc.

pseudomachine: a software computer, created to act as the universal machine that will run any program. You need another piece of software, an interface program peculiar to your particular computer, to translate source programs written in its native assembly language into p-code (the universal language) and the input to the pseudomachine. The pseudomachine was developed by Dr. Kenneth Bowles at the University of California at San Diego.

punch: 1: a paper or Mylar-tape perforator. 2: to record data on a paper or Mylar tape with a tape punch. 3: to record data on a magnetic-tape cassette.

punch card: a card punched with a pattern of holes to represent data. Punch cards are still used with large mainframes operating in the batch mode but are scarce in the world of mini- and microcomputers. Even the mainframe owners are replacing punch cards with magnetic disk and tape for a multitude of good reasons, such as storage space, speed, cost/bit, etc.

punch tape: a paper or Mylar tape about an inch wide and usually many feet long, in which data have been punched in code as a sequence of characters along the length of the tape. Each character is represented by a binary code of holes (or no holes) across the tape. The characters are usually encoded with a 7-bit ASCII code and an eighth parity bit. The tape is used to enter data and programs into a computer, using a computer-controlled tape reader, which may be a Teletype (TTY) or a high-speed tape reader (300 characters per second, for example). Punch tape is obsolescent.

purge date: a date written on a magnetic tape or disk to specify when it should be released for reuse, erasing, or overwriting.

quad: 1: four of anything. A quad two-input NAND gate IC contains four such gates. 2: (British): a cable consisting of two twisted-pair insulated wires in a protective jacket. 3: a typesetting space that is one en or more in width. Short for quadrat, a usually rectangular plot used for ecological or population studies.

quad center: in automatic typesetting, a command to cause a line to be printed in the center of the typeset line. *Example:* in the Intergraphics system, the quad code, qc, appended to the end of an input text line, will cause the line to be centered between the page margins.

quad code: in automatic typesetting, a control code inserted in an input manuscript to cause the typesetting computer to set a line flush left (quad left), flush right (quad right), or centered (quad center).

quadding: 1: filling in a typeset line with quads. 2: the quads used.

quad floppy-disk controller chip: a VLSI 40-pin DIP IC chip that supports two double-sided, dual-density disk drives. It provided 20:1 parts reduction over conventional controller boards.

quad left: in automatic typesetting, an end-of-the-line command that causes the line to be printed flush left. *Example:* in the Intergraphics system, the control code, ql, is appended to the end of an input text line.

quad right: in automatic typesetting, an end-of-the-line command that causes the line to be printed flush right. *Example:* in the Intergraphics system, the control code, qr, is appended to the end of an input text line.

qualification: in COBOL, the making of a name or other data item unique by adding IN or OF, according to defined rules and procedures.

qualifier: a name added to another to distinguish it from others having the same name. In computers, the name is usually a command or an instruction.

quasi-: a prefix meaning simulated. *Example:* a quasi-instruction, a synonym for a pseudoinstruction.

queue: 1: a waiting line controlled by a service mechanism. One enters at the tail of the queue, waits in line until one arrives at its head, gets serviced, and then leaves the queue. 2: a special-purpose one-dimensional array of data items awaiting processing in a computer, in accordance with an ordering scheme, defined as the queue discipline. The usual discipline is first in, first out (FIFO). *Example:* a supermarket checkout waiting line. Other queue disciplines are last in, first out (LIFO). *Examples:* a stack of dishes in a steam table or a program stack; and priority (VIP and the divine right of kings). There are row queues and circular queues.

queue discipline: the algorithm employed to determine how a queue is serviced.

quote: short for quotation mark.

QWERTY keyboard: the standard typewriter and video terminal keyboard layout, to distinguish it from some of the newer designs, such as the Dvorak keyboard, in which the most used letters fall under the fingers in "home row," the rest position.

ragged: in typesetting, unjustified.

ragged code: in automatic typesetting, a control code inserted in a line of input text to cause one of the margins to be unjustified (ragged). Possibilities are flush left/ragged right, ragged center, and ragged left/flush right.

ragged right-hand margin: an unjustified right-hand margin with the appearance of a typical typewritten page.

RAM: *See* **random-access memory.**

random-access memory (RAM): a memory organized and constructed in cells, each of which can be reached (accessed) directly, without going through other irrelevant cells first. In the microcomputer world, RAM means a semi-conductor, volatile, read/write memory used as a scratch pad for storage of input data, intermediate results, or program development, as opposed to ROM, PROM, EROM, EE-PROM, or EPROM, read-only memories used entirely for fixed program instructions or data tables and constants. A RAM may also contain output ports.

random-stroke writing: a graphics technique in which images are created on a CRT screen by drawing or scanning a straight-line vector between two selected points, as opposed to the raster-scan method. Circles and arcs are generated by a series of straight-line segments. DVSTs and calligraphic displays employ random-stroke writing.

range: all of the possible or allowed values of a function or variable.

rank: to order a set in ascending or descending importance.

raster: the displayed pattern of scanning lines covering the screen on a television receiver, monitor, or video terminal when the horizontal and the vertical sweep oscillators are functioning, with or without the video picture information to modulate the intensity of the electron beam. Displays that function this way are known as raster-scan units, as opposed to stroke equipments.

raster count: the resolution of a video display screen in terms of picture elements; horizontal count is across the width, and vertical count is from top to bottom.

raster-scan bit mapping: one of the three graphics technologies, with stroke system, and raster-scan conversion. The image is an *x,y* matrix of picture elements (pixels), stored as a complete frame, and must be refreshed at least 30 times per second to avoid flicker. The refresh rate is independent of image complexity, unlike stroke graphics.

raster-scan conversion: one of the three graphics techniques, in which a vector is converted into rectangular *x,y* coordinates for display by a raster-scan beam.

raster staircasing: in bit-mapped raster-scan graphics, a ragged effect created when a line is drawn with squares instead of small dots, due to low resolution.

raw data: ideally, data that have not been processed, filtered, or reduced in any way. Actually, analog data that have only been digitized, with negligible loss in precision due to A/D converter resolution or other errors, are normally considered raw.

reader: short for punch-tape reader or punch-card reader, obsolescent computer I/O units. *See* **punch card**; **punch tape**.

read head: the electromagnetic device that recovers (reads) data from a magnetic tape or disk. Usually, one head, the read/write head, reads and writes. Read head suggests that the two are separate, but that may not be so.

read in data: to transfer data from one unit to another. *Example:* to move a file from a floppy disk into main memory.

reading head: (British): a synonym for a read head, in magnetic recording technology.

read-only memory: a memory purposefully designed to be read only and never written to. Strictly speaking, ROMs, PROMs, EPROMs, EEPROMs, EROMs, and EAROMs are all read-only memories.

read or read out: 1: to determine the value of a register, flip-flop, input port, memory cell, etc. 2: to copy from one storage location into another.

readout: 1: a value read. 2: a display. 3: synonymous with read.

read rate: a measure of how fast the processor can input data from a peripheral device, in terms of the number of words, blocks, or fields read in a given time interval.

reconfigure: to alter the type, interconnection, priority, etc., of components in a computer system.

record: 1: a collection of related data items handled as a unit. 2: a subdivision of a file. 3: to enter data into a storage device. 4: in PASCAL, a data structure that may contain several related data items that are of differing types.

record blocking: the process of dividing a file of records into blocks of data that can be written to a magnetic medium in one operation.

record format: the prescribed arrangement and contents of the data in a record such that the processor can recognize and process it.

record gap: synonymous with interrecord gap; an unrecorded length of magnetic tape between records.

record head: a synonym for the write function of a read/write head.

recording density: the number of bits per unit length of linear track on a magnetic recording medium; synonymous with bit density.

record length: a measure of the size of a record, specified as the number of words or characters. On a floppy disk, a record may be 128 bytes by default. It may be defined to be any other length.

recoverable error: an error that is detectable and temporary and can be corrected later. Synonymous with soft error.

recovery: the process of returning to the status that existed before an error or some other undesirable event occurred.

recovery routine: a software program that does whatever is necessary to correct or minimize the effects of an error. Short for error recovery routine.

rectangle filling: in computer graphics, painting the inner area of a rectangle primitive shape with a tint of solid color, crosshatch, etc.

reduction: short for data reduction, the processing of raw data by scaling, averaging, limiting, applying reasonableness tests, organizing, tabulating, etc.

reel: a spool used in magnetic-tape transports or cartridges. Two are required for reel-to-reel transfers: a supply reel and a take-up reel.

reformat: 1: to format a data file again, changing the structure of a data item. 2: in word processing, to change one or more of the established format settings: left margin, right margin, paragraph indentation, line spacing, lines per page, etc.

refresh: to rewrite data continually into the storage elements of a dynamic register to prevent their loss.

refresh plane: synonymous with bit plane.

refresh rate: in computer graphics, the number of times per second that a given line or vector is redrawn. To avoid flicker, 30 times per second is minimum.

regenerate: to restore information in a volatile memory cell or on the screen of a CRT. The more popular term today is refresh.

register: a temporary storage or memory for digital data, usually composed of a number of flip-flops. A flip-flop is a 1-bit register.

relative unit space: in typesetting, a unit of space equal to $1/18$ of the typeface point size in use. *Example:* with 9-point characters, a unit space is $9 \times 1/18 = 1/2$ point $= 1/2 \times 1/72 = 1/144$ inch. Any space can be built up in increments of $1/144$ inch.

remote: describing equipment that is far away, at least in the next room or building, but often miles away and connected by telephone lines and modems.

remote batch processing: the processing of data received from remote terminals or computers, in the batch mode.

remote computer: a computer located at some distance from one or more of its input terminals and connected to it by a communications link, usually a modem and telephone lines.

remote device: a peripheral connected to a computer via a communications link, such as a radio data link or telephone lines.

remote job entry (RJE):   a term applied to a computer terminal or its required software that permits it to communicate over leased or switched lines with a mainframe computer operating in a batch mode.

repaginate: to renumber the pages of a document.

repeating key: any keyboard key that repeats its character or function automatically as long as it is held depressed. Synonymous with autorepeat key. On some terminals, all keys are repeating; on others, only certain ones.

repertoire: a complete set of possible operations or functions. As applied to computer instructions, synonymous with instruction set. (A musician's repertoire is a complete list of the pieces, compositions, etc., he is prepared to perform.)

replication: the duplication of one or more hardware units in a system for use as standby equipment in case the first unit fails.

report generator: a software utility program, part of an operating system, that produces reports on a printer or CRT. The user must define the format and detail of the input devices, files, data, output devices, etc., as inputs to the program before it can run successfully.

report-program generator (RPG):   a report-generator utility. *See* **report generator**.

rescue dump: a memory dump made to magnetic tape or disk for backup or comparison purposes, usually when the system has been acting up and trouble is anticipated.

reserve: 1: to restrict, as in a reserved word. 2: to allocate or assign, as in reserved areas of memory in multitasking or multiprogramming.

reset: 1: to change a computer, register, counter, or another device to its initial value, usually zero. 2: the RESET state of a device.

resident: residing in, pertaining to a computer utility program that processes a program for its own use, as opposed to cross-software products that run on a larger, host computer.

resident software: a general term for any resident program. *See* **resident**.

resolution: the number of addressable picture elements in a graphics display, measured in pixels. One graphics board provides a resolution of 768 horizontal by 512 vertical, corresponding to 393,216 memory locations for a memory-mapped display. Each location contains an 8-bit binary word that specifies one of 32 different colors to be displayed at one of eight different intensity levels.

resource: in a computer system with multiple users, a peripheral unit that must be shared.

response: the output characteristics of a system or device with time or frequency as a function of its input parameters. Two types of response define the performance of any system: its transient response, which is determined by testing its recovery from a step input; its steady-state response, which is determined by measuring its output amplitude and phase as the input frequency is varied over its operating range of values.

response time: the interval between the generation of the last character of a message at a terminal and the receipt of the character of the reply, including all delays within the terminal, along the network, and at the service nodes.

restart: to resume execution after an unplanned interruption, usually a power interruption or an error. Restart generally implies picking up where it left off, as opposed to a reset, which starts over at the beginning.

retrieval: as in information retrieval, the process, methodology, etc., of storing information such that it can be found again later with a minimum amount of time and effort. Very large data banks and computerized means of storing and retrieving the data are implied.

return-to-zero format (RZ): a format for representing serial binary data during transmission or recording; the signal or recording voltage returns to the logic 0 value after every 1 bit and stays there for each logic 0 bit. *See* **non-return-to-zero format**.

reverse line-feed: a characteristic of some high-speed printers that output a line-feed and then print from the right-hand margin back to the left-hand margin, as opposed to the normal line-feed and carriage return. Synonymous with bidirectional printing.

reverse type: white letters on a dark background; the typesetting equivalent of reverse video on a CRT screen.

reverse video: a synonym for inverse video, the preferred term.

rewind: in a reel-to-reel storage device, such as a magnetic or paper tape, to cause motion to fill up the supply reel, returning to the beginning-of-tape marker (in the case of magnetic tape).

rewrite: to record the same data again, usually after an error.

ribbon cable: a flat, multiconductor-insulated wiring cable commonly used for interconnecting printed-circuit (PC) boards and/or disk drives inside a small computer, word processor, or one of their peripherals.

right-justify: 1: to adjust the printing positions of the characters on a page to make the right margin even. 2: in the computer, to shift the contents of a register until the least significant digit is at a predefined position in the register. 3: to align characters horizontally to place the rightmost character of a string in a specified position. *See* **left-justified; left-justify**.

Example: given the following data list, 1.5, 1.001, 23.4567, 0.0991, assume an 8-bit data word. If right-justified, the computer will interpret the data as follows for an 8-digit data field:

```
0 0 0 0 0 1 . 5
0 0 0 1 . 0 0 1
0 2 3 . 4 5 6 7
0 0 0 . 0 9 9 1
```

robot: a machine or any other mechanical device that operates automatically with humanlike skill or "intelligence." Robots only look human in the movies or on TV. Robots are a large application area for computer systems.

robotics: the technology or science of designing and fabricating robots and their computer brains. Robotics is a blend of the older technologies of automatic control, numerical control, automation, and computer science in the form of artificial intelligence. The science-fiction writers, TV people, and marketers love robotics.

ROM: a read-only memory, one or more semiconductor memory chips. ROMs are produced and programmed in large quantities only (1000 or more) by a semiconductor manufacturer during fabrication. A read-only memory that is user programmable is called a PROM, EPROM, EROM, EE-PROM, or EAROM. ROM chips are used for program instructions and fixed data; you cannot write new data to a ROM. A number of ROM chips may be assembled into a larger memory on a printed-circuit card or board. ROMs are usually sized and sold by the number of words and the word size they store. *Example:* a ROM that stores 1024 8-bits words is a 1K × 8 ROM.

root: 1: the top of a hierarchical tree structure. 2: the base node of a structure diagram or another tree structure.

route: in local area networking, to pass a message along to an adjacent node.

row: a horizontal set of elements in a rectangular array or table.

RS-232C port: a serial input or output port designed, constructed, and operated in accordance with an EIA (Electronic Industries Association) data communications industry specification and standard, RS-232C. RS-232C serial interfaces are probably the most common lines of communication between a CPU and its video terminal and often between its printer and other I/O devices that may be located at some distance from the computer.

rubout: to erase electronically.

rubout character: a video or teletypewriter keyboard control character used to delete characters typed into a terminal buffer memory. Sometimes it's abbreviated to rub, labeled DEL or delete, even erase.

rule: in typesetting, a solid, continuous line, sometimes used to emphasize, outline, or separate areas on a printed page.

run: 1: to execute a computer program (or cause it to be executed). 2: a particular execution of a computer program.

runaway: describing an out-of-control situation in a physical system that departs from normal operating conditions for the unknown distant ones.

run time: the period of time when a program is actually executing on a computer or when it first starts to execute.

run-time library: a collection of software utility routines from which one or more may be called at run time to execute regularly supportive tasks, such as calling certain files from disk storage, supervising spooling operations to a line printer, etc.

S

satellite computer: a secondary or subservient computer connected to a central processor, perhaps for front-end or parallel processing.

save: to write a file from volatile RAM to semipermanent secondary storage, usually a floppy disk or magnetic-tape cassette.

scaling (graphics): changing the relative size of objects on the screen, thus affecting their orientation.

scan: 1: to examine sequentially, line by line, usually in a repetitive pattern. 2: in computer string handling, testing a string to determine if a particular substring pattern or character is present. 3: to traverse the inside surface of the screen of a television tube or video monitor CRT horizontally and vertically, spraying it with a beam of electrons, in order to create an image.

scanning rate: the speed at which a scan is conducted.

schema: in data-base management, a description of the structure of the data base.

scissor: in graphics, to delete an element in a display.

scope: short for oscilloscopes, the CRT test instrument used to display electrical waveforms and other time-dependent phenomena. Periodic events are shown as still pictures; aperiodic events can be captured if the CRT has a long-persistence screen or if special memory oscilloscopes are used.

scratch tape: a magnetic tape used for testing, intermediate results, or any other data not requiring permanent storage.

screen: 1: the visible end of a cathode-ray tube in a video monitor. 2: one page on a video terminal screen, usually 24 eighty-character lines.

screen context printing: a 1:1 mapping of the video terminal CRT screen to a hard-copy printer. Synonymous with screen dump.

screen dump: a 1:1 hard-copy printout of the displayed characters on a CRT screen. Synonymous with screen context printing.

screen editor: a word-processing software program used to change, add, delete, rearrange, and otherwise modify an entire screen of text characters, as opposed to a line editor that operates on a line at a time. Text editor is the general term that includes both line and screen editors. Screen editors are characterized by block move capability, in which whole paragraphs can be moved to a new place in the text, and by commands that can insert material from outside files.

screen generator: a utility used to facilitate the formatting and presentation of text data on a video display screen. A screen generator does the same job for CRT screen displays that a report generator utility does for printed hard-copy reports.

screenload: synonymous with screen, the text contents of one frame of a video display.

screen memory: the maximum number of characters that may be typed on the CRT screen at any one time. For a screen of 24 eighty-character lines, the screen memory is 1920 characters. If each character is 8 bits, that is 15,360 bits per screen.

scrog: (slang): to wipe out a memory or other electronic component, usually permanently. If it was temporary, it was only scrubbed.

scroll: to move an entire screen of characters as a frame, usually up or down, although some terminals scroll horizontally as well. This is an advantage for spreadsheet analysis with 132 columns, for example, since probably only 80 columns can be viewed at a time.

scrolling: the vertical movement of data displayed on a CRT or video terminal. A new line appears at the bottom for each line that disappears from the top, or vice versa.

scrub a memory: (slang): to lose all the contents of one or more locations, usually as a result of a power or equipment failure, but you can easily do it by overwriting if you are doing assembly-language work. If your memory gets scrubbed, you are all washed up until you write the information back in from a copy somewhere. The memory cells are normally not damaged; you have to scrog a memory to do that.

SDLC (synchronous data-link control): a communications protocol for the transfer of data between stations in point-to-point, multipoint, or loop arrangements, using synchronous data-transmission techniques.

search: the process of scanning a body of data in a systematic manner, looking for a particular value, string, symbol, or character. *See* **binary search.**

search and replace: a capability of some editors and word processors to go through a text, find each and every occurrence of a given word, phrase, or string, and automatically replace it with a new word or phrase. Synonymous with the "substitute" command in some word-processing systems.

search list: a list of directories (expressed as pathnames) that an operating system will search from top to bottom whenever it cannot find the file specified in a pathname with no prefix (some operating systems). *See* **pathname.**

search time: the time required to locate a particular data field in a storage device.

search window: an area of interest that is being scanned.

secondary sort: the second sort within the sorted items of a primary sort. *See* **primary sort.**

secondary storage: synonymous with bulk storage. The add-on memory peripheral units, usually magnetic disk and/or magnetic tape, capable of storing tens to thousands of times the data resident in main working memory. *See* **bulk storage.**

sector: a subdivision of a track on a magnetic disk. A track on a large 8-inch disk is divided into 26 sectors, whereas a smaller 5¼-inch disk has 18 sectors. Each sector, typically, holds one record or 128 bytes. *See* **track.**

secure system: an operating system in which one programmer's mistakes, a disgruntled employee, or a person with criminal intent cannot read or alter sensitive areas, make the system crash, or affect other processes.

seek: to move a magnetic disk read/write head to the proper track prior to a read or write operation.

segment number: a binary number defining a memory segment. The segment number is concatenated with a binary offset (the displacement within the segment) to form the physical address of the data.

seize: to acquire the use of or gain access to a dictation device or channel.

select error: an error message indicating that a tape-transport selection problem exists; perhaps no transport was assigned the programmed select code or the same code was assigned to more than one unit.

selective dump: a dump of only a portion of a memory or storage, as opposed to a dump of the entire memory.

Selectric: short for IBM's Selectric electric typewriter, a form of automatic impact printer. Selectrics use interchangeable spherical type fonts about the size of a golf ball for each character set. Many have been converted to computer-compatible, letter-quality automatic printers, using an added interface card.

self-clocking: describing binary codes that change state once per bit time (clock period), avoiding the requirement for a separate synchronizing clock signal. *Examples:* the Manchester phase-encoded codes.

self-diagnostic: a test program called and executed automatically when a fault is detected, as opposed to a manually initiated diagnostic routine.

semantic error: a programming error committed when an incorrect or ambiguous symbol is used or when a correct symbol is not used.

semantics: 1: the study of the meaning of words in a language. 2: the set of rules that describes what to expect when a particular programming-language construct is used. 3: the branch of linguistics concerned with the nature, structure, and, particularly, the development and changes in the meaning of speech forms, or with contextual meaning. *See* **semiotics**; **syntactics**.

semiautomatic: describing a process that is not totally automatic but instead requires intervention by a human operator.

semiotics: a general theory of language signs and symbols, especially the analysis of the nature and relationships of signs. Semiotics is normally divided into three subsciences: syntactics, semantics, and pragmatics.

sense: 1: to test the value of a system input. 2: the direction of a bipolar signal. 3: to detect an output of a device.

sensitivity: the magnitude of the ratio of an output variable expressed in one set of units to an input variable expressed in another unit. *Example:* a temperature transducer has a sensitivity of 1 millivolt per degree Celsius. Gain is a special case of sensitivity in which the input and output units are the same.

sensor: a generic term for an electrical measuring device that produces an output current or voltage proportional to and representative of a physical quantity being monitored, such as temperature, fluid level, altitude, etc.

separator commas: the commas that separate the variable values in a data file record; spaces may also be used for readability, but in long data files, they slow things down and take up a lot of disk space.

sequence: 1: the following of one element after another in logical, causal, or chronological order. 2: an ordered set of data or instructions.

sequence check: the test of an ordered set to see if it is in the specified order.

sequencing: causing a set of actions to occur in a predetermined order.

sequential: 1: synonymous with serial. 2: describing events that occur one after another, without appreciable overlap.

sequential access: a data-access method that requires searching through a potentially long series of irrelevant storage locations before getting to the desired data. Not random access. Synonymous with serial access. *See* **indexed sequential-access method**.

sequential file: 1: a file that can be accessed sequentially only. 2: a file with its key fields arranged in a sequential format.

serial: describing an operation conducted sequentially, in time and physical construction, as opposed to a parallel operation, in which more than one operation is conducted simultaneously or along parallel paths.

serial access: synonymous with sequential access.

serial printer: a mechanism in which characters are printed one at a time as the print head moves down a line of print, as opposed to a parallel or line printer, which prints an entire line at a time.

series: 1: a number of things or events arranged in some order and connected by a common characteristic. 2: in mathematics, an expression that is the sum of a large (sometimes infinite) number of subexpressions called terms, constructed in accordance with a common logic rule.

series connection: a connection of elements arranged such that the output of each device is connected to the input of the following unit.

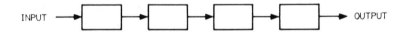

service full-duplex: *See* **full-duplex operation**.

service half-duplex: *See* **half-duplex operation**.

service program: a synonym for a utility.

service routine: 1: short for interrupt service routine. 2: a utility for an I/O device.

set a marker: *See* **text marking**.

set type: to arrange type characters for printing.

shared resources: a generic term referring to a common memory unit, file, printer, etc., that can be accessed and used by two or more computers or other devices.

sheet-feeder: a printer accessory that automatically feeds standard 8½-by-11-inch sheets of paper into the printer.

shield: a conducting jacket, usually of braided copper wire, placed around a wire or cable to protect it from induced or capacitively coupled noise voltages. One end of the shield must be connected to signal ground to be effective.

shielded cable: a cable that has a braided metallic jacket around the one or more wires inside to minimize electrical noise pickup; there may also be an outside sleeve of insulating material to keep the metal shield from shorting external circuits. When installed, the shield should be connected to electrical ground at one end only. *See* **coaxial cable**.

short: an accidental or intentional very low-resistance conducting path between two points in an electrical device or circuit, drawing a relatively high current and preventing the development of the normal output voltage. Short for short circuit.

short circuit: *See* **short**.

short out: to place a short across two points in an electrical device or circuit.

sign off: the last instruction from a remote terminal to a computer in a time-share system after a period of system use. The sign-off instruction is usually BYE or OFF.

sign on: synonymous with login or logon; the procedure or sequence of instructions that must be executed to gain access to and use a computer running in a multiuser mode or a time-share system.

simplex: describing a data channel that can transmit or receive, but not simultaneously.

simulate: to duplicate or represent the characteristics or behavior of one physical system with another more convenient, smaller, or lower-cost system for the purpose of studying it. *Example:* a circuit of resistors, capacitors, and inductances that simulate the characteristics of an electromechanical gun-firing servomechanism.

single-density disk: a floppy disk for single-density recording, to distinguish it from dual-density or double-density disks. You cannot use or read a double-density disk on a single-density drive. A single-sided, single-density disk stores less than 100,000 characters, whereas the dual-density, double-sided floppies store close to four times that amount.

single-line sort: a sort on a name, for example, or any single-variable list, as opposed to a multiple-line sort. *See* **multiple-line sort.**

single-sided disk: a disk in which information is recorded on just one of its two surfaces, as opposed to a double-sided disk. Single-sided and single-density go together; so do double-sided and double-density.

sink: the receiving end of a transfer through a medium. *Examples:* a current sink into which the current flows; a heat sink that absorbs the flow of heat from a power transistor. The opposite is the source.

slave: a device temporarily or permanently under the control of another device, usually a processor called the master or controller.

slave mode: the mode of operation of one computer acting as a slave to another, called the master or controller.

Smalltalk: a personal computer system designed in the 1970s at Xerox's Palo Alto Research Center to introduce computer concepts to children. It had a bit-mapped graphics display, a mouse, and a "modeless" environment. Some of Apple Computer's Lisa's advanced computer system features were inspired by Smalltalk.

smart: describing any device or equipment containing a microprocessor and memory, giving it some front-end processing ability. The opposite is a dumb device. Synonymous with intelligent.

smart dot-matrix printer: a printer that contains a microprocessor with several predetermined high-resolution character sets (fonts) of various typefaces in read-only memory. The font can be changed dynamically, as a program runs, to produce multifont pages. *Example:* italics can be embedded in ordinary pica text.

smart modem: a modem with autodial capability, plus other advanced features. A microprocessor communicates with the host processor.

SMD format: small magnetic-disk format, small magnetic-drive format.

soft: describing anything flexible, subject to change, or temporary. *Examples:* software, soft sectoring, soft errors.

soft carriage return: in word processing, a carriage return inserted in a line to break it at the end, but whose place may vary if the line is reformatted.

soft copy: any temporary nonprinting display of computer data, subject to change, that cannot be retained. Usually, it is on the CRT. *See* **hard-copy printout**.

soft error: a temporary error in a read or write transaction involving a magnetic medium such as a floppy disk or tape, but sometimes applied to semiconductor RAMs. The cause may be alpha radiation, static electricity, dust, etc. A soft error can be corrected by overwriting. A hard error cannot.

soft failure: 1: a failure that can be corrected without interrupting normal operation. 2: a failure that results in degraded but continuing operation.

soft hyphen: a hyphen inserted by a word processor to break a word at the end of a line; it is soft because if the line is reformatted the hyphen may appear at a different place or not at all. Contrast it with the hard hyphen, which is always inserted in a word at the same place, wherever it is in the line. *See* **hard hyphen**.

soft key: a key whose function and descriptive cap can be changed to implement a specialized user need. ***Examples:*** user-definable function keys on a video terminal.

soft-landing head: a feature of some floppy-disk drives. Recording heads literally fly on a cushion of air. When writing is complete, the head is not allowed to drop suddenly onto the magnetic coating. Instead, it is eased down to avoid damage.

soft sector: a floppy- or hard-disk sector created by software on a variable-size physical area of the disk, as opposed to a hard-sectored disk with the sectors delimited by holes through the disk.

soft space: in justifying (beautifying) a line, a space inserted to make the right margin come out where it should; if the line is reformatted, the space may not be required or may appear in a different place in the line.

software: one or more programs, procedures, and other documents involved in the operation and maintenance of a computer system. Program listings, floppy disks, paper-tape programs, a library of subroutines on magnetic tape, user and programmer manuals, and specifications are all software—not hardware or firmware. When a program is committed to ROM or PROM, it becomes firmware—usually. There is no standard, and some people call PROMs software.

software library: a file of procedures, routines, and programs for use as modular inclusions into other programs or saved for use at some later time.

solid-state switch: a switch implemented with field-effect transistors (FETs) or other semiconductor material, with no moving parts, as opposed to the old mechanical switch.

son: describing one or more file copies made from an original file or disk, which then became a father. If a son disk is copied, it then becomes a father and the father becomes a grandfather disk or copy. All copies may be modified over a period of time, so the copies may soon bear only a family resemblance.

sort: to divide items into groups in accordance with one or more preset rules. Types of sorts include alphabetic, numeric, alphanumeric, ascending, descending, primary, secondary, bubble, etc.

sort key: the basis, rule, or characteristic used to assign an item into a particular group in a sort routine.

sort menu: a menu listing the types of available sort programs in a given operating software system.

sort routine: a procedure that arranges a file of items in accordance with a rule or rules: alphabetically, ascending or descending numerical order, etc.

source: 1: the transmitting end of a transfer through a medium; the other end is the sink. 2: one of the three electrodes or terminals of a field-effect transistor; the others are the gate and the drain. The source is the origin of the charge carriers.

source computer: 1: a computer used to preprocess data at its source prior to transmission to a distant computer for further processing. 2: a preprocessor.

source deck: a set of punch cards that contains the instructions or statements to be input to an assembler, interpreter, or compiler. Synonymous with source pack.

source language: the language in which a programmer writes a program. Source code is then translated into object code or language, usually by a computer. The source language may be assembly or mnemonic symbolic language or one of the high-level languages, such as FORTRAN or BASIC. More often than not, the object code is a machine language of binary code.

source machine: the computer that assembles or compiles a program, as opposed to the object machine that runs the program.

source pack: a synonym for a source deck of punched cards.

source program: 1: a program of instructions written in a source code or language. 2: the program prepared by the programmer, as opposed to the object program produced by a computer.

space: in teletypewriter communications, the binary 0. Binary 1 is a "mark."

space bar: the space character bar on a video terminal or typewriter keyboard.

space character: the ASCII printable character that causes a printer to skip one character on a line and print a space. Synonymous with blank character.

span: the range of values between the highest and lowest in the set.

special character: a generic reference to a punctuation mark or symbol in a printing font or ASCII table.

specification: a formal statement of the requirements for an equipment or software document. It is often the only real definition of performance, speed, accuracy, environmental design, etc., and should be reviewed in addition to the marketer's brochures before buying anything.

spelling dictionary: a computer utility program that tries to match words in a text with its list of approved spellings. It then displays a list of possible replacement spellings for selection by the user.

spike: a sharp, peaked, short-duration voltage transient, a noise element.

spindle: the hub in a disk drive that holds and centers the disk. A dual drive has two spindles, giving rise to the practice of rating the market in numbers of spindles.

spindle hole: the large 1⅛-inch hole in the center of a floppy disk. The drive spindle slips through it to center the disk precisely in the drive. Synonymous with hub hole.

Spinwriter-type printer: a printer employing a thimble print head, similar to the NEC Spinwriter's. Spinwriter is a registered trademark of Nippon Electric Corporation. *See* **thimble.**

spooler: a software utility that temporarily stores a file for printing in a queue until the system or network printer is available.

spooling operation: the process of writing data into a holding ("spooling") area on a disk file for temporary storage until it can be output to an I/O device, such as a printer or magnetic-tape transport. Spooling areas are necessary because many users require the printer, and the computer generates the data much faster than the printer can handle it. There is no need to make the CPU sit there and wait.

spreadsheet: 1: the large ruled work sheets that bookkeepers and accountants use to spread out income, expenses, etc., by listing or posting them into categories in appropriate columns on the sheet. 2: the computer programs that effect the electronic equivalent, with automatic addition of column totals, cross-footing, etc. VisiCalc is a popular electronic spreadsheet. VISICALC™ is the registered trademark of VisiCorp.

sprite: a simple animated figure of computer graphics, like those in the Pac Man video game, that represents a man, object, animal, etc. A sprite is generally a block of pixels moved about a CRT screen with a joystick, trackball, or keyboard cursor key.

sprocket feed: a method of high-speed printer paper feed using sprocket wheels that engage holes along both edges of the paper, much as film is fed through a 35mm camera. Synonymous with tractor feed.

stand-alone computer: a general-purpose computer that operates by itself, not as a built-in dedicated component of a large system.

standard binary code: the representation of a quantity or character in the base-2 binary number system, as opposed to BCD, excess-3, or some other special-purpose binary code. Synonymous with straight binary.

standard interface: an interface built to a predetermined specification as to the number of interconnecting wires, their order, the voltage, impedance, or current levels, rise times, fall times, etc. The agreement is made to allow the equipment of different manufacturers to work together in a common system. An RS-232C serial interface is the prime example of a standard interface that allows almost all computers to communicate with terminals and with other computers, modems, printers, etc. The general-purpose interface bus (GPIB) was established to bring some commonality to digital instrumentation.

standby: 1: describing a mode in which an equipment is ready to be used but is not performing its full repertoire of operations, perhaps to save power. 2: describing a redundant equipment waiting to be used if another unit already in operation fails or must be shut down for maintenance, etc.

star network: in data transmission, a configuration in which the satellite equipments are connected radially to a central station.

star program: (British): one of those few programs that run perfectly on the first attempt.

start bit: one or more bits that precede the data bits in a character code during a serial transmission. The start bit, or bits, identifies the next bit as the first data bit in the character. The last bit in the character is usually followed by one or more stop bits.

star topology: a local network configuration; stations are on lines radiating from a common center where a computer acts as master network controller, managing common resources, preventing collisions, etc.

static: 1: pertaining to a fixed or stationary condition; not dynamic or changing. 2: short for static electricity, an induced electrical charge on a person or equipment during dry weather. 3: electrical noise on a radio signal, due to a variety of possible causes.

status: the condition or state of a variable, bit, or device, including a computer.

status line: in some screen editors and word processors, the first displayed line at the top of the video screen, above the text to be edited, showing the edit mode, last command, command menu, etc.

stop bit: the last bit in a serially transmitted character, usually to a tele-typewriter or video terminal, using a UART (universal asynchronous receiver-transmitter) and an RS232-C serial link. In some codes, two stop bits are used. *See* **start bit**.

stop code: a word-processor command embedded in the printable characters of a document, causing the printer to stop. Stop codes are inserted in a text at a point where a type-font change is desired, for example.

storage: synonymous with memory. *See* **store**.

store: 1: to put a computer word into memory. 2: (British): memory, based on the use of the word by Babbage, the inventor of a mechanical calculator that had a memory he called the "store." 3: one specified area of memory dedicated to a particular use.

stored program: the set of instructions and the fixed data in memory that define the operations to be performed by the computer.

straight binary: the ordinary binary base-2 number system code, as opposed to the many other binary codes, such as reflected binary, BCD, BCO, excess-3, offset binary, etc. Synonymous with standard binary.

streaming tape drive: a digital cartridge drive that verifies data "on the fly" with a read-while-write check as it is recorded; that is, what is written is immediately read back in real time and tested. In addition, a check character is appended to each blockette for data verification during read passes. Conventional tape drives must verify data by backspacing a whole block or by rewinding the reel or cartridge. Streaming tape drives are used for backing up floppy-disk drives or Winchester hard disks.

strike control: in some word processor/printers, the capability to make a variety of print character strikes: single, double, triple, boldface, shadow-print, etc.

strikeover: the usual way of correcting minor typos by typing the correct letter over the wrong ones. Sometimes called the exchange mode.

striking out: overprinting a hyphen, a slash, or a backslash through text characters. *Example:* -------, / / / / / / / /, \\\.

string: 1: a linear sequence of characters, usually alphanumeric, but many strings contain punctuation symbols and other ASCII characters with special meaning. 2: any set of data items arranged in a sequence according to a rule.

string constant: a string that always has the same value wherever and whenever it appears in a program. Synonymous with string literal.

string literal: a string constant. As opposed to a string variable, a string literal will remain constant. *Example:* the string variable NAME$ could be BILL, MARY, PETER, JANE, etc. HELLO, a string literal, never changes.

string variable: a string that will change when a program runs. *Example:* the string variable MONTH$ may be JANUARY, MARCH, NOVEMBER, etc., at various times when the program is executed.

stroke: 1: in computer graphics, a line or arc created by a movement of the CRT electron beam from some starting point *A* to an end point *B*, as opposed to a line created by a raster-scan beam. *See* **raster**. 2: to draw a line using stroke graphics techniques.

stroke graphics: one of the three basic types of graphics display systems; the others are raster-scan bit mapping and raster-scan conversion. *See* **stroke**.

stroker: a display terminal that uses vector-refresh graphics, synonymous with stroke graphics.

stroke system: one of three graphics technologies (with raster-scan conversion and raster-scan bit mapping). Lines are drawn as vectors, using point coordinates and point-to-point plotting. Lines are moved or rotated by recalculating their end points only and sweeping directly to them.

structured object: in graphics, an object constructed from other modular shapes, usually primitives, such as lines, arcs, circles, triangles, polygons, etc.

stylus: a pen-shaped, hard-pointed tool used for indicating a point on a CRT screen.

subscript: a character written next to but slightly below another. *Example:* the number 3 is a subscript to the variable a_3.

superior number: in typesetting, a superscript. In automatic typesetting, a control code is inserted in the typewritten input manuscript to specify a superior number, avoiding the time-wasting reversing of the platen to type it above the line. A subscript is an inferior number.

supermicro: a microcomputer implemented with one of the 16/32-bit microprocessor families. *Example:* Motorola's MC68000 series or National Semiconductor's NS16000. Microcomputers have much greater computing power and speed than the 8-bit versions and are displacing minicomputers in small-scale business and scientific applications.

superscript: a character written next to but slightly above another. Mathematically, a number superscript generally indicates exponentiation, or raising the number to a power. *Example:* the 2 in a^2 is a superscript.

support: to enable the use of. An operating system supports a PASCAL compiler if this program can be loaded and run on the system.

support software: system software that will run on your machine in support of you. Not applications software that you write.

suppression: the inhibition of the printing of certain characters, usually zeros, as leading or trailing characters in a field.

swap: a memory-management software operation in which data are transferred between secondary storage files and main high-speed memory, in either direction, generally overwriting some other no longer needed program when swapped in. Swapping should be transparent to the user, making main memory appear to be many times its actual size. Fast swapping may involve an intermediate cache memory.

swap out: *See* **swap**.

swapping mode: in some compilers, an operating mode in which the whole compiler is never brought into main memory from disk at any time. Instead, a required portion ("phase") is swapped in, used, and then swapped out, to be replaced with the next phase. *See* **swap**.

switch: 1: a device for turning on or off or directing an electrical signal, usually by direct manual operation, as opposed to a relay that can be actuated by remote control. 2: a modification to an operating system command or argument. In Data General's RDOS Command Line Interpreter, a switch is delineated by a right slash (/), followed by the switch itself. *Example:* QPRINT/ BEGIN=20/COPIES=2 modifies the normal print operation to cause the printer to start at page 20 instead of page 1 and to make an additional copy.

switched-message network: a data communications network in which all users can send or receive messages to/from any other user.

symbol: a representation of something by reason of relationship, association, or convention.

sync: short for synchronize.

sync character: a character, usually the first character in a word, group, or message, sent by a transmitting equipment to be recognized by the receiver as the start of the transmission.

synchronization: 1: the process of synchronizing. 2: the state of being synchronized.

synchronize: to cause to happen at the same time: "Gentlemen, synchronize your watches." The presence or absence of actuating voltages on the data input to a flip-flop, for example, must be carefully synchronized, by good system design, with the arrival of the clock pulse.

synchronous: occurring at the same time. Most events within a computer are synchronous with the system clock, the basic timing reference for the system. Many I/O units are asynchronous (not synchronous) unless provided with the system clock signal for synchronization.

synchronous transmission: communications between digital devices in which data are transferred at a predetermined rate, with the transmitter and the receiver synchronized by connecting the transmitter's clock to the receiving equipment so that the two have a common system clock. Synchronous transmission removes the requirement for start/stop bits, words, or characters, thus providing greater speed and efficiency than asynchronous transmission but at the cost of the additional clock wire or wires.

syntactical: referring to the syntax rules of a language.

syntactical error: synonymous with syntax error.

syntactics: the branch of semiotics dealing with the formal relationships of signs and symbols to one another, apart from their use or external reference.

syntax: 1: the arrangement of words as elements in a sentence to show their relationship to one another. 2: the organization and relationships of word groups, phrases, clauses, and sentences. 3: sentence structure.

syntax error: a programming error in which a statement or command was written using improper syntax for the language, as opposed, for example, to an error in logic. Synonymous with syntactical error; the shorter form is preferred.

SYSGEN: an acronym for a system-generation program. *See* **system-generation program**.

system: a set of interdependent devices, procedures, programs, rules, etc., organized to form an integral entity to achieve a specified result.

systematic programming: synonymous with structured programming, the more popular term.

system-command language: synonymous with job-control language. An operator can create a sequence of instructions that will cause the system to perform an entire series of specified tasks later.

system design: in the data-processing world, the process of determining in detail the exact operational requirements of a system, specifying its file structures and I/O formats and relating each to management tasks and information requirements.

system-generation program: an operating system support software program that customizes the monitor program to fit the user's requirements. SYSGEN programs work in an interpretive mode, offering menus of device selections, protocols, etc. TRSDOS calls its system-generation program CONFIG.

system integrator: a person who assembles components made by diverse manufacturers into a working system. He must specify and purchase, or make, interfaces between equipments not particularly designed to work together. Often he must write or obtain special software, too.

system monitor: an operating system utility program that provides I/O driver programs for the front-panel switches and status indications of a computer.

system resident: pertaining to program instructions and data stored in semiconductor ROM, as opposed to media-resident software stored on removeable media, such as tape cassettes, floppy disks, etc.

system root directory: the top or root of a directory tree. All other directories are subordinate. *See* **directory**; **tree**.

systems analysis: the definition of problems, objectives, priorities, and constraints of a system for the purpose of developing or improving it. The task involves the examination, definition, and evaluation of the component parts, equipments, and subsystems and their interrelationships. A systems analyst must also identify and rank costs, advantages, and disadvantages and sometimes make schedule estimates for viable alternatives.

systems analyst: one who does systems analysis, usually with special training and experience in that area. He generally is the interface between the users and the designers and programmer. In small companies he may do the hardware design and the programming as well. This practice is common in companies whose products involve embedded microcomputers; one person must understand both hardware and software.

system software: the operating system software, the collection of programs provided by the computer manufacturer to facilitate the use of a computer.

T

tab: 1: a synonym for a label. 2: an operator-selected point on a line of text in a typewriter or word processor. When a tab key is depressed, the cursor (or typewriter carriage) advances to the next tab position to the right of its current position. Tabs are used in typing tables and other columnar documents.

table: a set of data items stored in memory in a form convenient for easy and quick access by the CPU.

table lookup: a programming technique used to find the value of a function stored in a table of values for the function, using one or more of the arguments of the function to enter the table. ***Example:*** given a stored table of sines for angles in 1-degree increments, to get the sine of 30 degrees (the argument), the table would be entered at 30 to retrieve the sine, 0.5000.

tail: a software flag at the end of a list.

take-up reel: the reel on which tape is wound during a reel-to-reel transfer. The other reel is the feed reel.

tape: 1: short for magnetic tape, punch tape, paper, tape, or Mylar tape, all used for secondary storage of programs and data, although the last three are becoming obsolete. 2: short for program tape.

tape cassette: a digital or audio magnetic-tape cassette used in conjunction with a cassette tape transport for bulk storage. It is microcomputer-compatible and one of the least expensive methods.

tape deck: a magnetic-tape drive plus its required electronics. Synonymous with tape transport. The tape transport is more likely to be free-standing, and the tape deck is usually part of a larger recording assembly.

tape drive: an electromechanical component of a tape transport, cartridge, or cassette player. The tape drive moves the tape past the read/write head. Loosely, a tape transport.

tape mark: a predefined bit pattern recorded on a magnetic tape to indicate a significant event: the end of a data block, the last record for a given date, etc.

tape punch: an obsolescent device for punching or perforating paper or Mylar tape for the storage of computer data. The tape punch may be operated manually "off-line," or it may be a computer-controlled I/O unit to punch automatically an output tape.

tape reader: an obsolescent input device used to enter data or programs into a computer. The tape reader uses paper or Mylar tapes punched by a tape punch. Each serial character along the length of the tape is represented by binary-coded holes (or no holes) across the width of the tape. The holes are detected by mechanical or photoelectric devices and are converted into corresponding electrical pulses that can be input to the computer for processing.

tape skip: a command from a computer's tape-drive controller to the transport mechanism to pass a tape section containing a hard error, erasing as it goes.

tape speed: the linear speed of a magnetic tape past the read/write head. Tape speed is usually measured in inches per second (ips); 25 ips is typical.

tape transport: synonymous with magnetic-tape drive.

target: synonymous with object, in general. *See* **target computer**.

target computer: the computer for which a machine-language object program is assembled, using cross-software on a host computer. *Example:* a machine-language program for an Intel 8048 microcomputer is assembled using a cross-assembler loaded into a Data General Eclipse minicomputer. An 8048 assembly-language source program is entered into the Eclipse, which then produces the machine code and assembly listing. The Eclipse is the host; the 8048 is the target.

target language: the object language of a language-translation program.

task: a job or a program that a computer working in a multitasking, multi-processing, or multiprogramming environment may be scheduled to run.

task scheduler: a software utility routine in some operating systems for multitasking environments. The task scheduler resolves contentions between requests for the services of the CPU. Maybe it should be called the CPU scheduler.

tele-:   a prefix meaning at a distance. *Examples:* teletype, telecommunication, teleprinter, teleprocessing.

telecommunication: communication over a long distance, usually implying the use of radio or telephone-line links.

telecomputing: computing at a distance, usually with a modem over telephone lines. The connection may be to another computer, a data bank, or a videotex or teletext service.

teleprinter: synonymous with teletypewriter.

teleprocessing: remote processing by means of terminals and/or computers connected by telephone lines and modems or by a radio link. The reference is normally made in connection with videotex services, in which a terminal is connected via a modem to a remote computer or data bank.

teletext: the broadcast or cable television screen messages provided by some services, particularly in Europe and the United Kingdom where they do not have to compete with the regular commercials.

Teletype (TTY): an obsolescent electromechanical computer I/O terminal originally designed for the telegraph application. It has a full ASCII keyboard and a slow-speed hard-copy impact printer; it may also have a tape punch and tape reader, also slow speed. Teletypes were used to program, enter, and store programs and data, test and debug, and print out results during a program run under computer control. Teletype is a trademark of the Teletype Corporation.

Teletype code: synonymous with Baudot code. Teletype is a registered trademark of the Teletype Corporation. Not all Teletypes use the 5-bit Baudot code, let alone all teletypewriters. The older machines did.

teletypewriter: the generic name for the older electromechanical remote typewriters, characterized by the Teletype machine. Teletype is a trademark of the Teletype Corporation.

Telex: an international teletypewriter network similar to TWX.

Telex roll: a continuous roll of printer paper, 8½ inches wide, so called because teletypewriter and Telex machines use it.

template: 1: a plastic stencil used to draw electronic or logic hardware or software flowchart symbols. 2: a subset of a string, used during search operations to find all strings containing the substring.

temporary storage: 1: CPU registers and flags that change during the course of a program. 2: memory location reserved for intermediate results that are overwritten with new data when the old data are no longer needed. 3: scratchpad memory.

tera-: a prefix meaning a million million, 10^{12}.

teracycle: a million million cycles per second, 10^{12} hertz.

terminal: 1: an I/O unit for operator and programmer interface with the computer. Terminal literally means end, and in this case it is the front end (the input) and the back end (the output) of the system. *Examples:* teletypewriters, video terminals. Usually, a terminal is a two-way device, with a keyboard manual input and a printer or a video display output. 2: an electrode or connector on a semiconductor or other electronic device, such as a diode, transistor, FET, or integrated circuit.

text editor: a software utility program designed to facilitate the editing of text characters. A text editor is usually a line editor, operating on a line at a time, as opposed to a screen editor, which can move or delete whole paragraphs at a time. *See* **editor.**

text enhancement: the ability of some printers to emphasize selected characters in a text by darkening them with multiple overstrikes, compressing more than the normal number into a line, expanding character width or height, etc. The penalty is slower printing speed.

text justification: *See* **justify; left-justified; left-justify; right-justify.**

text marking: an editing feature of most word processors. An invisible position "marker" is inserted at the cursor position as a delimiter when a "set marker" command is executed by keyboard strokes. If a marker is set at each end of a sentence to mark and delimit it, it may then be deleted or moved by subsequent commands.

text screen dump: a printed facsimile of a video terminal CRT screen by a hard-copy printer, just as it appears on the screen. Synonymous with screen dump.

thermal printer: a printer technology that prints characters by burning a dot matrix into special heat-sensitive paper. Thermal print heads have wire electrodes that burn off a light, metallized surface layer, exposing a dark background.

thimble: the print wheel or head on a thimble printer, a form of impact printer. A character set is arranged around the open end of a cup-shaped print head resembling a big thimble. The NEC Spinwriter (a trademark of Nippon Electric Corporation) uses thimbles.

thimble printer: a type of impact printer employing a thimblelike print head or type font. *See* **thimble**.

thin space: one of the three standard spaces in typesetting: the others are the em space and the en space. A thin space is equal in width to the punctuation marks (period, comma, semicolon, etc.) of the font being used. The actual width depends on the point size and particular font.

tilde: the symbol, ~, used in some mathematical and foreign language documents.

tilt: in typesetting, the slant upward and to the right on some typefaces.

time-share network: one of several commercial computer services that uses a large mainframe on a time-share basis to serve many clients simultaneously. The user accesses the computer (which is usually in a distant city), using his own telephone and a compatible acoustic coupler with modem connected to a suitable terminal. The terminal includes a keyboard for manual program and data entry, a printer, and/or a video display.

time sharing: the simultaneous use of one computer's resources by several users, usually in a time-sharing network in which they are connected to a large mainframe computer by telephone lines. The term may also apply to a multiuser environment in a single building. Even microcomputers work so fast that one CPU can be used by several operators or I/O units, apparently simultaneously. Actually, the CPU services each user one at a time for short periods (sometimes seconds or less). Hopefully, each user feels as if he has the undivided attention of the CPU, since usually the delays are hardly noticeable, except during the rush hour on a big time-share service computer.

tint: one of the possible variations in a color.

toggle: 1: a terminal key that actuates a function when pushed once, then deactivates the same function when pushed the second time, alternating on and off, etc. 2: to use or operate a toggle key or switch.

token packet: a standard data block circulated from station to station in a bus network using token passing to avoid collisions between stations. *See* **token passing**.

token passing: a local area network control technique that avoids collisions on bus networks. A "token packet" is continuously circulated along the bus line from one station to its adjacent neighbor when the bus is idle and no stations are transmitting. To use the bus, each station must wait for the token to arrive, "seize" the token, and remove it from the bus. When the transmission is complete, the token is put back in circulation. All other stations must remain quiet until the token arrives.

tool: anything that makes a job easier, whether hardware or software. *See* **software tool**.

top-of-form control: an off-line control switch on a high-speed printer. When pushed, the paper will advance to a preset position or distance below the top of the page. The control is used to advance the paper to a convenient spot for tearing off the finished printout while leaving it in the right position to start the next printout.

touch pen: *See* **touch screen**.

touch screen: a computer input technique in which two infrared transmitters (one horizontal, one vertical) are used to create an invisible x,y grid on the viewing screen of a CRT. When a stylus is touched to a point on the screen, its location is detected by mutually perpendicular beams, generating computer-compatible position numbers.

TPI: tracks per inch, a measure of magnetic-media density.

trace: 1: a printed sequential listing on a printer or video terminal of the actual program line number executed by a debug program during software development as the program runs. Most likely, it is not the desired sequence. 2: the pattern on the face or screen of a oscilloscope.

track: a separate recording path on a magnetic tape or disk.

trackball: a video game input device that acts as a transducer to change rotational displacements into proportional electrical outputs. It consists of a spherical ball, about 2 to 3 inches in diameter, with only the top of the sphere projecting out of its mounting assembly. The ball is rotated fore-aft, left-right, or some combination of the two with the fingers of one hand, displacing electrical potentiometers, producing the voltages.

track density: the number of tracks per unit length, measured perpendicularly to the direction of the individual tracks for tape or radially for disks and diskettes. Track pitch is the inverse of track density.

track pitch: the centerline-to-centerline distance between two adjacent tracks on a magnetic recording medium such as a tape, drum, or disk.

tractor edges: pertaining to computer-printer paper with punched holes spaced about ½ inch apart along both edges of the paper to engage the sprocket pins in a sprocket-feed (tractor-feed) printer.

tractor feed: a printer paper-feed mechanization; sprocket pins in both ends of the platen engage holes along both ends of the paper, providing a positive paper feed that prevents lateral wander of the paper roll, an affliction of some friction-feed paper handlers.

trailing zeros: zeros filled in to the right of nonzero digits in a number to fill out a field of fixed length. *Examples:* for an 8-character field, 13400000, 444.6700, .8300000.

transaction: in business data processing, the sequence of steps that follows the input of one data record and continues until any immediately connected output has been completed.

transceiver: a combination transmitter and receiver in the same package or equipment. In the computer world, it usually refers to an electronic circuit that serves as a line driver (transmitter) and line receiver, connecting the computer to a peripheral over a relatively long bidirectional bus line.

transducer: in general, a conversion device that produces an output in one form in response to an input in a different form. Usually, it converts pressure, temperature, fluid level, volume, or some other physical parameter into an electrical signal output. Synonymous with sensor.

transformation: mathematical modifications of the coordinates of a graphic image (shape, volume, etc.) in order to translate, rotate, or rescale it.

transformer: an alternating-current device used in computer power supplies to reduce 115 volts 60 Hz to a lower, more suitable level for rectification and conversion to low-level DC voltage.

transient: 1: a short-period undesired fluctuation in voltage or current. 2: describing an effect that is short term and dies out quickly, as opposed to "steady-state" effects that are longer term.

transistor: a semiconductor device for controlling the flow of current between two terminals, the emitter and collector, by means of variations in the current flow between a third terminal, the base, and one of the other two.

translate: 1: to transform statements from one language into another without significantly changing the meaning, whether the language is spoken, written, or one of the programming languages. 2: in graphics, to move an object without rotation, from one point on the screen to another: horizontally, vertically, or some combination of the two motions.

translation time: the time at which the program is assembled, interpreted, or compiled from a source language to a machine code.

translator: a generic term for an assembler, compiler, or interpreter that converts a source language into an object language.

transmission rate: the speed at which data can be or is sent over a channel of communication. Transmission rate is measured as the number of data elements sent in a unit time interval, expressed as baud rate or bits, characters, words, records, etc., per second. Synonymous with data transfer rate and transmission speed.

transmission speed: *See* **transmission rate**.

transparent (to the user):   a term widely applied to a number of computer situations, describing an operation executed in the background with negligible effect on an operator performing a task in the visible foreground.

transportability: synonymous with portability.

tree: 1: a graphic network representative of the hierarchy of a program, directory, organization, etc., resembling the root structure of a tree. 2: a branching logic structure having only one path from the root to any leaf node.

troubleshoot: to hunt for the cause of a hardware or software problem so that it may be eliminated.

truncate, truncation: to lop off. The discarding of one or more least significant digits in a number (or bits in the binary number resulting from an arithmetic operation) whether by choice or accident. *Example:* 123.496 is truncated to 123.4 for four significant digits, causing a 0.1 truncation error. For accuracy it should have been rounded to 123.5.

trunk: 1: a transmission-line channel or circuit between offices, switching centers, and subscribers. 2: a synonym for bus.

tube: short for cathode-ray tube, the screen of the video monitor.

turtle: in LOGO graphics, a small, triangular CRT screen cursor that a child can learn to rotate and translate independently. The turtle is moved with a handful of simple commands, creating little drawings as it goes. ***Example:*** a FORWARD 6 command moves the turtle six units in the direction the turtle is "facing." RIGHT and LEFT are rotate commands; LEFT 90 turns the turtle's nose 90 degrees.

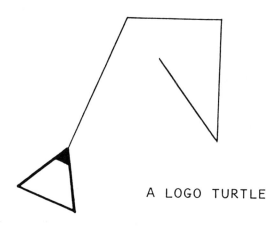

A LOGO TURTLE

turtle geometry: a new field of mathematics that studies and defines the figures of turtle graphics.

turtle graphics: the line figures created when a turtle is moved around a CRT screen with LOGO commands.

typeset: produced by a typesetting system.

typesetter: a machine used to set magazine and book quality type. *See* **set type**.

type wheel: a print head, such as a daisy wheel, that has all of the characters for a given character set or font. Type wheels are mechanically designed to snap in or out of place for quick installation and removal in the printer mechanism. They must be changed to substitute one typeface for another.

U

UART: universal asynchronous receiver-transmitter, an integrated-circuit support chip for microprocessors, designed to interface a word-parallel processor, controller, terminal, or any other digital system to a bit-serial communications link. A UART is bidirectional and programmable. The number of start and stop bits, odd or even parity, and other details of the serial data protocol are set by the programmer. Usually, the UART is initialized as a part of the housekeeping chores early in the program run.

ultra-large-scale integration (ULSI):   a term used to describe the chips designed and fabricated with focused ion beams (FIB), achieving densities far beyond VLSI (very large-scale integration), the limit of photolithographic resolutions. A million-bit random-memory chip should be available in 1985; 4 megabits by 1990.

ultraviolet-erasable: describing an EROM or EPROM (erasable read-only memory or erasable programmable read-only memory). The IC device is programmed electrically by storing an electric charge on an insulated gate. The charge may be erased using an ultraviolet light to cause the charge to leak off because of photoelectric effects. Ultraviolet light is the invisible portion of the electromagnetic frequency spectrum just beyond the visible violet wavelengths.

unary operator: an operator that needs only one operand. *Example:* the arithmetic sign + is a unary operator, assigning a positive value to the variable A in the expression, $A = +1$. However, the same + symbol becomes a dyadic operator in the arithmetic expression, $A = B + C$, where it indicates addition of the variable B to the variable C.

unbundled: not bundled. Referring to the practice of selling a complete computer system, hardware and software (a bundled package deal only), and not allowing the customer to buy parts of the system, especially the software, from another vendor.

underscore: synonymous with underline; printing a continuous line below a line of text characters.

undo: a common feature of some text and screen editors. If you blunder and inadvertently delete a section of text, you can execute the "undo" command to annul the last deletion and restore the text to its preedited condition.

universal product code (UPC): the familiar supermarket bar code. *See* **bar code**.

UNIX: one of the mostly widely used operating systems for computers. UNIX is a development and trademark of Bell Laboratories.

unjustified: not justified; ragged. *See* **justify**.

upload: to transfer data from an I/O peripheral device into the computer. To transfer data from the computer to the I/O unit is to download it.

USART: universal synchronous and asynchronous receiver-transmittter, a microcomputer or microprocessor interface chip that can be programmed under CPU control to act in either a synchronous or an asynchronous mode to convert a bit-serial data word to a word-parallel format for computer input. It is bidirectional and can also convert the parallel output of the CPU to serial format and transfer the data to the I/O unit.

USASCII: synonymous with ASCII: the United States of America Standard for Information Interchange, rarely used in this country.

user mode: the mode of operation of an MC68000 or similar computer that has two modes: supervisory and user. The supervisory state has privileged instructions that are denied use by the user. A computer is in the user mode when a user is programming or running a program, although any user interrupt will cause it to trap to the supervisory state to handle the interrupt processing.

USRT: a universal synchronous receiver-transmitter, a digital data communications peripheral device that operates in a synchronous mode with its processor.

utility: a software program prepared by a computer manufacturer or software vendor, generally as part of an operating system, to perform any of several useful timesaving tasks. *See* **librarian; task scheduler.**

validate, validation: to test a data item to determine if its value is reasonable.

validity: correctness; the presence of true data, not noise.

variable: the name assigned to a computer quantity that can or will assume different values during a program run. The name should be a mnemonic to be easily associated with the function of the variable. *Example:* TNX for the tangent of angle X.

variable leading (rhymes with bedding): a feature of some of the newer printers that can vary the leading (the spacing between lines of print). Conventional line spacing is 6 lines per inch; with some newer printers, you can select up to 10 lines per inch. On the NEC Spinwriter or Toshiba printers, leading can be varied in increments of 1/120 inch.

VDI: video or visual display input, video display interface, virtual device interface.

vector: 1: a pointer to an address in memory. 2: an identifier address assigned to an interrupting I/O peripheral device to identify it from all the other possible interruptors on the bus. When the unit interrupts, it places its vector on the computer I/O bus. The CPU uses the vector to branch to the location in memory of the interrupt service routine for that device. 3: a physical quantity having both magnitude and direction. 4: loosely, a one-dimensional array.

vector (graphics): a directed line segment defined by specifying its end points only. It is drawn by the electron beam when it moves directly between the start and end points.

vector graphics: one of three main computer graphics technologies, along with raster-scan bit mapping and raster-scan conversion. Vector graphics is synonymous with stroke graphics or stroke system; all figures are drawn with vectors.

vector mode: in computer graphics, the manner in which the location of a vector to be drawn is referenced: in absolute coordinates (absolute mode); relative to some point (relative mode); as an increment (incremental mode).

verify: to test a transmitted block of data by a bit-by-bit comparison with the original message to detect errors. Usually, the computer does the verification, especially when the data are input from a magnetic tape or disk.

vertical redundancy checking (VRC): in a block parity having both vertical and horizontal dimensions, the parity check (odd or even) in the vertical.

video: 1: describing the range of television frequencies used to transmit the picture, as opposed to the audio frequencies, which carry the sound. 2: describing a terminal that employs a cathode-ray tube (CRT) to display data. 3: relating to picture information, as in video tape or video disk.

video attribute: one of the special qualities that can enhance or emphasize the characters printed on a video terminal, such as blinking, inverse video, half brightness, underlining, etc.

video bandwidth: the frequency range or response of the video amplifier, measured between the two points on a frequency vs. amplitude response curve where the amplitude has decreased -3 dB from the 0-dB passband line.

videodisc: an alternate spelling of video disk. *See* **video disk.**

videodisc technology: a developing secondary storage technology consisting of one or more optical disks in a compatible drive mechanism. Each aluminum disk spins at 1300 rpm in the drive made by Storage Technology Corporation. Present disks are read-only and incapable of erasure. Erasable versions are in development. Systems are priced over $100,000 now, but this technology may be the wave of the future. The Japanese and others are working on competitive versions, and prices are bound to come down with time. *See* **optical disk.** Also seen as video disk. See **video disk.**

video disk: a synonym for an optical disk, an aluminum platter about the size of a 33¹/₃-rpm audio record, but used with an optical drive to store up to 4 billion characters of read-only computer data. That is 40 times what a typical 7-inch reel of magnetic tape can hold and 1.5 times the amount you can store on an entire magnetic-disk drive. One square inch of its surface can hold 25 copies of *Gone with the Wind*. It is an emerging technology. Optical disks cannot be erased. The data are recorded with a laser that melts tiny pits in the aluminum surface. Another laser reads the data by sensing changes in reflectivity between the pitted (digital 1s) and nonpitted (digital 0s) surfaces. *See* **videodisc technology.**

video-display processor: a graphics controller that generates a composite video signal with the right electrical characteristics to drive a standard color TV receiver. It is used in low-end home computers with game-playing capability.

videographic: pertaining to graphics display on a video monitor, whether in black and white or in color.

video plane: a synonym for a bit plane or memory plane in bit-mapped computer graphics systems.

videotex: one of the television information services, more popular in Europe and the United Kingdom than in this country; a two-way interactive form of graphical communication. In the typical videotex system, a terminal connects the user to a central host computer via ordinary telephone lines and a modem. By making choices from menus, the user can send or receive messages, do electronic banking, read news reports, perform stock transactions, shop, retrieve information from data banks, etc., all for an initiation fee and monthly connection-time billings.

viewdata: pertaining to one of the interactive information services using telecommunications between a computer and one of the remote data bases available to public access. Synonymous with videotex.

viewport: the screen of a CRT in computer graphics. Its local coordinates show only a portion of a total picture in "world coordinates," which could require several viewports to display it all.

virtual: apparent, not absolute, actual, or real. *See* **virtual address; virtual memory**.

virtual address: a symbol used as part of a valid address but not necessarily designating an actual location. In paged or segmented addressing, the address within the page, which becomes the real or absolute address when the page or segment register number is added to it.

virtual machine: 1: a computer that can simulate the operation of another by executing its instruction set. 2: a computer simulated in software that is loaded and run in a larger machine. 3: a computer with a virtual memory.

virtual memory: a memory-management approach developed by a group of researchers at Manchester University in England in the 1950s. With virtual memory, the user considers the main high-speed memory and the slower secondary or bulk-storage drum or disk memories as a single large address space. Memory is divided into logic pages, which are then fetched from the peripheral storage when needed and returned when no longer required. The whole operation is transparent to the user, who can write very large programs far in excess of his main memory without a care in the world.

visual attribute: synonymous with video attribute.

visual display unit (VDU): a generic term for a video terminal.

VLSI: very large-scale integration; 10,000 or more devices on an integrated-circuit chip.

voice-grade: pertaining to a communication channel normally or historically used to transmit audio tones for telephone conversations and therefore somewhat restricted in frequency response, as opposed to leased-line data channels with a broader response. The frequency bandwidth is about 0 to 3000 Hz.

volatile: describing a memory that must be refreshed constantly to retain its data. Synonymous with dynamic. The opposite is static or nonvolatile.

W

wait list: (British): a synonym for a queue.

wand: a hand-held device used in optical-character-recognition equipment. *See* **OCR wand**.

warm boot: a computer start-up with the disk operating system already in semiconductor RAM after a previous cold boot by a bootstrap loader.

warm start: synonymous with warm boot.

Winchester drive: a hard-disk drive technology with extremely high reliability, with wide applications in small to medium-size computer systems. The essence of Winchester technology is a nonremovable head-to-disk assembly (HDA) sealed from outside air. Disks, read/write heads, and the head actuator operate in a contamination-free environment. A closed-loop filter equalizes pressure, and an absolute-recirculation filter traps all particles 0.3 microns or larger. Head crashes caused by dust and dirt are all but eliminated because the disk is protected from the external air with all its contaminates (cigarette smoke could be hazardous to the health of other disks). The read/write head floats and literally flies on a cushion of air 20 microinches from the magnetic-oxide-coated surface, permitting very high data-bit and track densities. The head rest on a silicone-lubricated landing pad during starts and stops. Winchesters require no preventative maintenance.

window: a specified block of lines in a program being edited. The lines in the window are in main memory, where they may be examined on the CRT. The rest of the program outside the window is not in main memory but still in secondary storage on disk or diskette. The purpose of window-mode operation is to ration memory when there are multiple users vying for the computer's resources. A specified block of contiguous memory locations, if an assembly-language editor is being used.

window (integrated software): an independent display area or rectangle on a video-display screen. The aspect ratio and size may be user-defined in some systems. Splitting a screen into three or four windows, each having its own independent function, such as spreadsheet analysis, word processing, etc., is a key feature of Lisa and the integrated software approach.

windowing: the ability to divide a CRT screen into several unrelated, independent displays, simultaneously operating as if they were separate pieces of paper on a desk.

window mode: *See* **window.**

wire-wrap: a popular and reliable solderless method of wiring between interconnection pins on computer backplanes, motherboards, and other assemblies. The pins are square shaped, and several turns of the stripped ends of the interconnecting wires are wound tightly around them by preprogrammed machines or manually by an operator with a hand "gun."

word: a group of bits assembled for a specific purpose, treated as a unit, and stored together in the same memory cell or register. *Examples:* a data word, an address word, an instruction word.

word processor: a computer dedicated to preparing, editing, formatting, reproducing, and storage of text.

word serial: a parallel data-transmission mode in which words are sent out in serial fashion, one after another, on a bus system.

word-wrap: a feature of some word processors that automatically keeps track of the spaces between words on a line, and if a word is incomplete at the end (and would therefore have to be hyphenated), the computer moves the entire word to the next line. This, of course, makes the right-hand margin temporarily ragged, but that is taken care of when the text is right-justified later.

work area: an area of random-access memory reserved for scratch-pad and other temporary-storage uses.

work disk: a disk copied from the distribution disk, which is the original disk that the software vendor delivers with the user's manual; whenever you receive a distribution disk, it should be copied right away to make a work disk for everyday use. The distribution disk should be stored in a safe place not exposed to temperature extremes or strong magnetic fields.

work file: in UCSD PASCAL, a temporary working copy of the program being modified with the text editor. The compiler takes its PASCAL program statements from the work file when the R(un) and C(ompile) commands are used.

working directory: a directory file used as a reference point within a directory tree in a computer operating system. *See* **directory tree.**

working memory: the high-speed semiconductor memory of the computer, comprised of the CPU temporary-storage registers and main memory, as opposed to its bulk-storage (secondary-storage) memory (disks, tape, etc.) on which files and programs not currently in use are stored.

work space: a synonym for work area.

workstation: 1: any computer terminal at which work is conducted. 2: in the evolving concept of the "office of the future," one of the input/output terminals designed for one or more individuals to access and use the shared resources of the system and to enter and retrieve information from its archives, files, and data banks. As a minimum, it consists of a desk and chair, a keyboard, and a video display.

world coordinates: in computer graphics, coordinates in an imaginary total "picture" for which data is available in the computer. The world coordinate grid may be 2 to 10 times larger than the device coordinates used for the screen (viewport). In other words, the screen at any time shows only a portion of the total world picture.

wraparound: 1: on a video screen, the continuation of a line of more than 80 characters that overflows onto the next line. 2: the overflow of characters from the bottom of the screen that is scrolled, overwriting data at the top of the new screen.

write: 1: to copy data from one storage location to another, for example, to a main memory location from a CPU register. After the write operation, the data remain in the source register, and any old data in the destination register are overwritten with the new data. 2: to transfer data resident in a computer to an external I/O device, such as a printer, magnetic floppy disk, or Winchester hard disk.

write head: an electromagnetic device in a magnetic disk, tape, or cassette drive that converts electric-current changes into magnetic flux to record data on the surface of the magnetic medium.

write operation: pertaining to an instruction or a procedure that executes the write function. *See* **write.**

write-over mode: in a word processor, the operational mode in which text characters are replaced by overwriting, as opposed to the insert mode in which inserting new characters in a line pushes the old ones down the line without losing or replace them. Synonymous with substitution mode and exchange mode in some systems.

writing head: synonymous with write head.

xerography: a process for reproducing graphic material. A lens system projects an image on a rotating mirrorlike surface that has been electrostatically charged. The drum and image rotate past a bath called the "toner," containing a black resinous powder. The charged characters pick up the toner particles, which are then offset (transferred) to any paper material as a copy.

XY plotter: a plotting device that plots a function $y = f(x)$ in rectangular coordinates, usually under computer control.

yoke: an electromagnetic deflection coil wrapped around the neck of a cathode-ray tube to steer the electron beam in television receivers, monitors, oscilloscopes, logic analyzers, and other test equipment.

Z

zap: 1: to destroy accidentally, usually by overheating. 2: to erase, especially a large area of a file. 3: (British): to program one or more locations in a fusible link PROM.

zero fill: to fill out a character, word, or memory location with zeros; the opposite of zero compression.

zero lead (rhymes with sled):   in automatic typesetting, a command inserted before a quad code to cause the line following the quad code to be on the same line; i.e., to inhibit a line feed. *Example:* in the Intergraphics system:

Name	Address	Telephone Number
{zl} {ql}	{zl} {qc}	{zl} {qr}

zero-level address: an immediate address.

zero suppression: synonymous with zero compression or elimination.

zoom: in computer graphics, to simulate on the CRT screen the effect of a TV or motion picture camera zoom lens, in which the image size can be continuously varied but will stay in focus at all times, giving the impression that the camera is moving toward or away from the object.

Appendix A

Printers

If I had to choose between a line printer and magnetic-disk storage, I'm not sure which it would be. For most applications, the absence of either would be a real handicap. If you do your own programming or modify purchased routines, the lack of a printer can cost hours of copying from the CRT screen. If you're a businessman, lack of a printer will deny you some of the most timesaving and valuable uses for your already expensive computer system: word processing, printing mailing lists, addressing envelopes, etc.

To aid you in dealing with the specialized world of printer language, the following abbreviated glossary is included.

automatic sheet feeder: a printer support mechanism that automatically feeds standard 8½-by-11-inch paper sheets into a printer, in lieu of continuous rolls or fanfold paper. Synonymous with cut-sheet feeder.

background print spooler: a software utility that outputs to a line printer (a spooling operation) when the foreground (higher-priority) programs or users do not require the line printer. The printer-spooler program works in the background in batch mode, queuing up printer jobs until the resources are available, and then runs the printer until all jobs are complete.

backspace character: a control character received by the printer from a controlling computer, causing the printer to backspace one character.

ball-point print head: a printer mechanism that uses a turret to rotate four miniature ball-point pens (red, blue, green, and black) into the writing position. A head controller coordinates horizontal print head movements with the paper-advance mechanism that manages vertical motion of the paper to print text or graphics in color or black on white.

band printer: a high-speed printer of fully formed characters mounted on a rotating band. Band printers can output at rates of hundreds of lines per minute.

blank character: a character that will produce a blank or space when transmitted to a printer or CRT. Same as space character.

buffer memory: a computer outputs characters to a printer at a rate much faster than any printer can operate. Therefore, characters are stored temporarily in the printer's buffer memory until the machine is able to print them. They are then replaced with other characters waiting to be printed.

Centronics interface: the most popular parallel interface for printers. It is a de facto standard, just as the RS-232C is the serial input standard.

chain printer: a printer in which the links of a revolving chain carry the type slugs.

character matrix: the matrix of dots used to print one character in a dot matrix. Typical character matrices are 5×7 and 7×9 dots.

character printer: a device that prints one character at a time, as opposed to a line printer, which prints an entire line of characters at one time.

character set: the collection of upper- and lower-case alphabetics, numerals, punctuation marks, and other symbols in the repertoire of a printer. The size and design of a character set constitute what is called a font in the printing industry.

columns of print: the maximum number of characters that can be written in a single printed line by a given printer. Confusing, what? A printed line is, of course, a row. But the term had its origin with the 80-column Hollerith (IBM) card, in which each character to be printed was punched vertically as a number of holes in one column of the card.

correspondence quality (of a printer): a marketing term for a print quality better than dot matrix, implying that it is also better than the competition's letter-quality characters.

CR: the carriage-return character.

cut-sheet paper: the ordinary 8½-by-11-inch sheet of paper, as opposed to other printer paper forms: continuous roll, fanfold, tractor-edge, etc.

daisy: short for daisy wheel or daisy-wheel printer.

daisy wheel: a print head in the form of a plastic disk with fully formed type characters at the end of arms radiating from the center of the disk, like daisy petals, forming a flat type wheel. On a given daisy wheel, all characters have the same font. But daisy wheels are designed to be interchangeable with other wheels having different typefaces.

(Courtesy of Inmac.)

daisy-wheel printer: a type of printer mechanization that employs a daisy-wheel print head. *See* **daisy wheel.**

dot matrix: a technique used by some printers to form characters, such as alphabetics, numerals, and punctuation symbols. The dots necessary to form the character are selected from a rectangular array of dots, usually 5×7 or 6×8.

dot-matrix character: a character printed by selecting the appropriate dots in a rectangular array (matrix) to form the desired pattern. The following figure shows dot-matrix characters. *See* **fully formed character; matrix.**

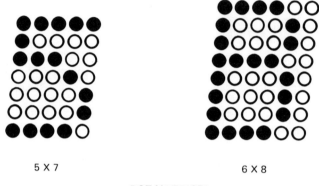

5 X 7   6 X 8

DOT MATRICES

dot-matrix printer: a mechanism that prints dot-matrix characters. Several types of print mechanisms are used.

drum printer: a high-speed printer mechanism that uses a cylindrical drum embossed with fully formed type characters. As the drum rotates at high speed, a computer-driven hammer strikes the paper from behind at the exact instant the desired character on the drum passes the position at which the letter is to be printed. There is a complete set of characters for each character position in the line. Each character set is embossed in a circumferential track in a plane perpendicular to the axis of rotation of the drum, one parallel track for each character in the line. The hammer traverses axially down the cylinder as it rotates, printing at high rates.

dumb dot-matrix printer: a printer capable of printing just a single fixed-character set, usually a low resolution 5×7, rather than many different fonts, changed under software control. *See* **smart dot-matrix printer.**

duty cycle: the percentage of time a printer is designed to operate continuously without pause. A printer that types for 1 minute and rests 3 minutes has a 25% duty cycle.

electrographic printer: a synonym for an electrostatic printer.

electrosensitive printer: a nonimpact dot-matrix printer that prints characters by burning dots into a special paper. The electrosensitive print head vaporizes dots of a light-colored, metallized coating so that a dark paper base shows through. Also called an electrostatic printer.

electrostatic printer: *See* **electrosensitive printer.**

elite: a common type character design and font, more delicate than pica, that prints at 12 pitch (12 characters per inch).

ESC: the escape character, a nonprinting control character for video terminals and printers.

fanfold paper: a continuous-feed form paper for a printer, usually high speed. As it runs out of the printer and into a receiving tray or basket, it piles itself neatly into pages, folding alternately at perforations at the top and then at the bottom of each page.

font: the size, shape, and design of a print-character set.

font-editor utility: a software program that facilitates the design of user-defined characters for computer displays having dot-addressable character cells.

form-feed character: a nonprinting control character transmitted by the computer to a printer to advance the paper form or roll.

form stop: a mechanical device that stops a printer when the paper runs out.

fully formed character: a solid character similar to one produced by a type-writer, as opposed to a dot-matrix or a seven-segment LED character.

impact printer: a printer that prints when the appropriate key strikes an inked ribbon against the paper, as opposed to one using other principles of operation, such as heat.

ink-jet printer: a printing technology using a print head that sprays dots of colored or black ink under computer control to form text characters or graphics images. (The Irwin/Olivetti JP101 printer sprays a fine powder instead of a liquid.) Ink-jet printers are quiet and highly reliable, with no moving parts. Best yet, multiple fonts are implemented with software.

italics: a type style with characters that slant up and to the right. Italics are used for emphasis: to catch your eye. *These words are set in italics.*

jet printer: short for ink-jet printer.

letter quality: describing a printer that types fully formed characters, as opposed to dot-matrix letters and numbers used by the lower-cost printers.

line-feed character: a nonprinting control character transmitted by a computer to a printer or video terminal to cause the cursor (and with it the line where ensuing characters are printed) to move to the next line.

line-feed code: a nonprinting control character that specifies the number of line feeds between each line to be printed by a line printer.

line printer: a computer peripheral device that prints an entire line of characters simultaneously, as opposed to a serial or character printer that prints only one character at a time. A line printer is a high-speed printer.

line spacing: the number of lines per inch of text. Spacing may be single, one and a half, double, or triple, as in typewriters, as well as half for subscripts and superscripts. Standard single spacing is six lines per inch; double spacing is three lines per inch.

listing: a program list, a computer printout of a list of statement numbers, statements, object codes, data, errors, etc., for a program or a part of it.

matrix: 1: an orderly rectangular array of elements. The plural is matrices. 2: an *n*-dimensional by *m*-dimensional rectangular array of numbers that may be added, multiplied, or inverted using specified rules of manipulation called matrix algebra. Computers were made for matrix manipulation and vice versa.

matrix printer: *See* **dot-matrix printer**.

microball-point pen: one of the small ball-point pens used in the turret of a ball-point print head. *See* **ball-point print head**.

multifont: describing a print head having more than one character set, usually with a different typeface, such as italics or Greek alphabet. Such a head is most useful when one typeface, such as italics, is embedded in a page of ordinary text.

OCR character: a printed character having a specified size, shape, and form readable by automatic optical-character-recognition equipment.

on line: a printer ready to accept characters under computer-program control is said to be "on line." Most printers have ON-LINE switchbuttons that are pushed to place the printer on line or to take it off line.

pagination: in computers, the arrangement and number of pages in memory, if the memory is paged; in publishing, the act of numbering the pages in a book.

pica: a common type font that prints at 10 pitch (10 characters per inch), larger than elite. Pica is a popular portable typewriter font.

pin feed: a commonly used technique and implementation to align and feed a continuous roll of printer paper by means of sprocket wheels at both edges of the form. Pins located around the circumference of the sprocket wheels engage uniformly spaced guide holes in the paper. Synonymous with sprocket feed and tractor feed.

pin feeder: a common pin-feed mechanization in automatic printers. *See* **pin feed**. Synonymous with sprocket feeder and tractor feeder.

pin-feed paper: fanfold or business-form paper with sprocket holes for paper feed on both sides.

pitch: the number of print characters per inch; common typewriter values are 8, 10, and 12 pitch, that is, 8, 10, and 12 characters per inch. Typesetters use a completely different type-sizing system based on a relative scale of 72 points per inch. Type size is measured in points, not pitch.

platen: the backing, usually a cylindrical roller of hard rubber or similar material, placed behind the paper in an impact printer. Each key strikes the paper, resting firmly against the platen.

printer: a typewriterlike computer peripheral that produces a hard-copy paper printout of computer data under the control of a central processor. There are all kinds: high-speed, line, character, impact, daisy-wheel, thermal, etc.

printer selector switch: in computer systems having more than one printer available, a mechanical switch is sometimes used to select the active machine. Sometimes PC-board-mounted DIP switches are used.

printer spooler: a disk area reserved for buffer storage of printing jobs that are queued up, awaiting printer availability.

printer terminal: a computer I/O unit with a keyboard for input and a printer for hard-copy output. They are widely used by time-share services, such as General Electric, which connect hundreds or thousands of users to a large mainframe through the use of acoustic couplers, modems, and telephone lines. In this application, hard-copy printouts are highly desirable, often mandatory.

print head: the part of a printer mechanism that puts the character on the paper.

print-head slew rate: the rotational speed at which a circular print head, such as a daisy wheel or thimble, can advance a new character into printing position.

printout: 1: the hard-copy print of computer data by a printer under CPU control. 2: to output computer data to a printer.

print wheel: the element containing the type font in an automatic printer or typewriter.

RS-232C port: a serial input or output port designed, constructed, and operated in accordance with an EIA (Electronic Industries Association) data communications industry specification and standard, RS-232C. RS-232C serial interfaces are probably the most common lines of communication between a CPU and its video terminal and often between its printer and other I/O devices that may be located at some distance from the computer.

serial printer: a mechanism in which characters are printed one at a time as the print head moves down a line of print, as opposed to a parallel or line printer, which prints an entire line at a time.

smart dot-matrix printer: a printer that contains a microprocessor with several predetermined high-resolution character sets (fonts) of various typefaces in read-only memory. The font can be changed dynamically, as a program runs, to produce multifont pages. *Example:* italics can be embedded in ordinary pica text.

space character: the ASCII printable character that causes a printer to skip one character on a line and print a space. Synonymous with blank character.

special character: a generic reference to a punctuation mark or symbol in a printing font or ASCII table.

Spinwriter-type printer: a printer employing a thimble print head, similar to the NEC Spinwriter's. Spinwriter is a registered trademark of Nippon Electric Corporation. *See* **thimble.**

spool: an acronym for simultaneous peripheral operations on line. *See* **spooling operation**.

spooler: a software utility that temporarily stores a file for printing in a queue until the system or network printer is available.

spooling operation: the process of writing data into a holding ("spooling") area on a disk file for temporary storage until it can be output to an I/O device, such as a printer or magnetic-tape transport. Spooling areas are necessary because many users require the printer, and the computer generates the data much faster than the printer can handle it. There is no need to make the CPU sit there and wait.

sprocket feed: a method of high-speed printer paper feed using sprocket wheels that engage holes along both edges of the paper, much as film is fed through a 35mm camera. Synonymous with tractor feed.

strikeover: the usual way of correcting minor typos by typing the correct letter over the wrong one. Sometimes called the exchange mode.

tab: an operator-selected point (or points) on a line of text. When a tab key is pressed, the cursor (or carriage on a typewriter) advances to the next tab position to the right of its current position. Tabs are used extensively in typing tables or other columnar documents.

text enhancement: the ability of some printers to emphasize selected characters in a text by darkening them with multiple overstrikes, compressing more than the normal number into a line, expanding character width or height, etc. The penalty is slower printing speed.

thermal printer: a printer technology that prints characters by burning a dot matrix into special heat-sensitive paper. Thermal print heads have wire electrodes that burn off a light, metallized surface layer, exposing a dark background.

thimble: a replaceable type font used by the NEC (Nippon Electric Corporation) Spinwriter printers and typewriters. The small-diameter, low-mass, specially reinforced plastic print element looks like an oversized sewing thimble, with up to 128 characters arranged around the perimeter of the opening. To change the character set, change the thimble, of which many types are available. Spinwriter is a trademark of NEC.

top-of-form control: an off-line (*see* **on line**) control switch on a high-speed printer. When it is pushed, the paper will advance to a preset distance below the top of the page. The control is used to advance the paper to a convenient spot for tearing off the finished printout.

tractor edges: pertaining to computer-printer paper with punched holes spaced about ½ inch apart along each edge of the paper to engage the sprocket pins in a tractor-feed printer paper mechanism.

tractor feed: synonymous with pin feed and sprocket feed.

TWX: a teletypewriter network operated by Western Union with real-time, two-way printed communication between subscribers, mainly corporations and government agencies. Telex is similar but international.

typeset: produced by a typesetting system.

type wheel: a print head, such as a daisy wheel, that has all the characters for a given character set or font. Type wheels are mechanically designed to snap in or out of place for quick installation and removal from the printer mechanism. They must be changed to substitute one typeface for another.

Appendix B

Table of Powers of 2

2^n	n	2^{-n}
1	0	1.0
2	1	0.5
4	2	0.25
8	3	0.125
16	4	0.062 5
32	5	0.031 25
64	6	0.015 625
128	7	0.007 812 5
256	8	0.003 906 25
512	9	0.001 953 125
1 024	10	0.000 976 562 5
2 048	11	0.000 488 281 25
4 096	12	0.000 244 140 625
8 192	13	0.000 122 070 312 5
16 384	14	0.000 061 035 156 25
32 768	15	0.000 030 517 578 125
65 536	16	0.000 015 258 789 062 5
131 072	17	0.000 007 629 394 531 25
262 144	18	0.000 003 814 697 265 625
524 288	19	0.000 001 907 348 632 812 5
1 048 576	20	0.000 000 953 674 316 406 25
2 097 152	21	0.000 000 476 837 158 203 125
4 194 304	22	0.000 000 238 418 579 101 562 5
8 388 608	23	0.000 000 119 209 289 550 781 25
16 777 216	24	0.000 000 059 604 644 775 390 625
33 554 432	25	0.000 000 029 802 322 387 695 312 5
67 108 864	26	0.000 000 014 901 161 193 847 656 25
134 217 728	27	0.000 000 007 450 580 596 923 828 125
268 435 456	28	0.000 000 003 725 290 298 461 914 062 5
536 870 912	29	0.000 000 001 862 645 149 230 957 031 45
1 073 741 824	30	0.000 000 000 931 322 574 615 478 515 625
2 147 483 648	31	0.000 000 000 465 661 287 307 739 257 812 5
4 294 967 296	32	0.000 000 000 232 830 643 653 869 628 906 25
8 589 934 592	33	0.000 000 000 116 415 321 826 934 814 453 125
17 179 869 184	34	0.000 000 000 058 207 660 913 467 407 226 562 5
34 359 738 368	35	0.000 000 000 029 103 830 456 733 703 613 281 25
68 719 476 736	36	0.000 000 000 014 551 915 228 366 851 806 640 625
137 438 953 472	37	0.000 000 000 007 275 957 614 183 425 903 320 312 5
274 877 906 944	38	0.000 000 000 003 637 978 807 091 712 951 660 156 25
549 755 813 888	39	0.000 000 000 001 818 989 403 545 856 475 830 078 125
1 099 511 627 776	40	0.000 000 000 000 909 494 701 772 928 237 915 039 062 5

Hexadecimal Arithmetic

Addition Table

0	1	2	3	4	5	6	7	8	9	A	B	C	D	E	F
1	02	03	04	05	06	07	08	09	0A	0B	0C	0D	0E	0F	10
2	03	04	05	06	07	08	09	0A	0B	0C	0D	0E	0F	10	11
3	04	05	06	07	08	09	0A	0B	0C	0D	0E	0F	10	11	12
4	05	06	07	08	09	0A	0B	0C	0D	0E	0F	10	11	12	13
5	06	07	08	09	0A	0B	0C	0D	0E	0F	10	11	12	13	14
6	07	08	09	0A	0B	0C	0D	0E	0F	10	11	12	13	14	15
7	08	09	0A	0B	0C	0D	0E	0F	10	11	12	13	14	15	16
8	09	0A	0B	0C	0D	0E	0F	10	11	12	13	14	15	16	17
9	0A	0B	0C	0D	0E	0F	10	11	12	13	14	15	16	17	18
A	0B	0C	0D	0E	0F	10	11	12	13	14	15	16	17	18	19
B	0C	0D	0E	0F	10	11	12	13	14	15	16	17	18	19	1A
C	0D	0E	0F	10	11	12	13	14	15	16	17	18	19	1A	1B
D	0E	0F	10	11	12	13	14	15	16	17	18	19	1A	1B	1C
E	0F	10	11	12	13	14	15	16	17	18	19	1A	1B	1C	1D
F	10	11	12	13	14	15	16	17	18	19	1A	1B	1C	1D	1E

Multiplication Table

	2	3	4	5	6	7	8	9	A	B	C	D	E	F
2	04	06	08	0A	0C	0E	10	12	14	16	18	1A	1C	1E
3	06	09	0C	0F	12	15	18	1B	1E	21	24	27	2A	2D
4	08	0C	10	14	18	1C	20	24	28	2C	30	34	38	3C
5	0A	0F	14	19	1E	23	28	2D	32	37	3C	41	46	4B
6	0C	12	18	1E	24	2A	30	36	3C	42	48	4E	54	5A
7	0E	15	1C	23	2A	31	38	3F	46	4D	54	5B	62	69
8	10	18	20	28	30	38	40	48	50	58	60	68	70	78
9	12	1B	24	2D	36	3F	48	51	5A	63	6C	75	7E	87
A	14	1E	28	32	3C	46	50	5A	64	6E	78	82	8C	96
B	16	21	2C	37	42	4D	58	63	6E	79	84	8F	9A	A5
C	18	24	30	3C	48	54	60	6C	78	84	90	9C	A8	B4
D	1A	27	34	41	4E	5B	68	75	82	8F	9C	A9	B6	C3
E	1C	2A	38	46	54	62	70	7E	8C	9A	A8	B6	C4	D2
F	1E	2B	3C	4B	5A	69	78	87	96	A5	B4	C3	D2	E1

Table of Powers of 16_{10}

16^n	n	16^{-n}
1	0	$0.10000\ 00000\ 00000\ 00000 \times 10$
16	1	$0.62500\ 00000\ 00000\ 00000 \times 10^{-1}$
256	2	$0.39062\ 50000\ 00000\ 00000 \times 10^{-2}$
4 096	3	$0.24414\ 06250\ 00000\ 00000 \times 10^{-3}$
65 536	4	$0.15258\ 78906\ 25000\ 00000 \times 10^{-4}$
1 048 576	5	$0.95367\ 43164\ 06250\ 00000 \times 10^{-6}$
16 777 216	6	$0.59604\ 64477\ 53906\ 25000 \times 10^{-7}$
268 435 456	7	$0.37252\ 90298\ 46191\ 40625 \times 10^{-8}$
4 294 967 296	8	$0.23283\ 06436\ 53869\ 62891 \times 10^{-9}$
68 719 476 736	9	$0.14551\ 91522\ 83668\ 51807 \times 10^{-10}$
1 099 511 627 776	10	$0.90949\ 47017\ 72928\ 23792 \times 10^{-12}$
17 592 186 044 416	11	$0.56843\ 41886\ 08080\ 14870 \times 10^{-13}$
281 474 976 710 656	12	$0.35527\ 13678\ 80050\ 09294 \times 10^{-14}$
4 503 599 627 370 496	13	$0.22204\ 46049\ 25031\ 30808 \times 10^{-15}$
72 057 594 037 927 936	14	$0.13877\ 78780\ 78144\ 56755 \times 10^{-16}$
1 152 921 504 606 846 976	15	$0.86736\ 17379\ 88403\ 54721 \times 10^{-18}$

Table of Powers of 10_{16}

10^n	n	10^{-n}
1	0	1.0000 0000 0000 0000
A	1	0.1999 9999 9999 999A
64	2	0.28F5 C28F 5C28 F5C3 $\times 16^{-1}$
3E8	3	0.4189 374B C6A7 EF9E $\times 16^{-2}$
2710	4	0.68DB 8BAC 710C B296 $\times 16^{-3}$
1 86A0	5	0.A7C5 AC47 1B47 8423 $\times 16^{-4}$
F 4240	6	0.10C6 F7A0 B5ED 8D37 $\times 16^{-4}$
98 9680	7	0.1AD7 F29A BCAF 4B5B $\times 16^{-5}$
5F5 E100	8	0.2AF3 1DC4 6118 73BF $\times 16^{-6}$
3B9A CA00	9	0.44BB 2FA0 9B5A 52CC $\times 16^{-7}$
2 540B E400	10	0.6DF3 7F67 5EF6 EADF $\times 16^{-8}$
17 4876 E800	11	0.AFEB FF0B CB24 AAFF $\times 16^{-9}$
E8 D4A5 1000	12	0.1197 9981 2DEA 1119 $\times 16^{-9}$
916 4E72 A000	13	0.1C25 C268 4976 81C2 $\times 16^{-10}$
5AF3 107A 4000	14	0.2D09 370D 4257 3604 $\times 16^{-11}$
3 8D7E A4C6 8000	15	0.480E BE7B 9D58 566D $\times 16^{-12}$
23 8652 6FC1 0000	16	0.734A CA5F 6226 F0AE $\times 16^{-13}$
163 4578 5DBA 0000	17	0.8877 AA32 36A4 B449 $\times 16^{-14}$
DE0 B6B3 A764 0000	18	0.1272 5DD1 D243 ABA1 $\times 16^{-14}$
8AC7 2304 89E8 0000	19	0.1DB3 C94F B6D2 AC35 $\times 16^{-15}$

References

This dictionary is, for the most part, original material expressed in the author's own words. The raw material for some of the definitions was gleaned from numerous fragmented glossaries. In just about all of these cases the words have been changed to make the definition easier to understand, more accurate, or simpler in structure. Some had to be brought up to date or tailored to microcomputer usage.

1. *The Random House Dictionary of the English Language*. New York: Random House.

2. Flores, Ivan. 1960. *Computer Logic*. Englewood Cliffs, N.J.: Prentice-Hall.

3. Motorola. 1975. *M6800 Microprocessor Applications Manual*. Motorola Semiconductor Products, Phoenix, Ariz.

4. Intel. 1974. *MCS-40 User's Manual for Logic Designers*. Intel Corporation, 3065 Bowers Avenue, Santa Clara, Calif.

5. Murphy, John S. 1958. *Basics of Digital Computers*. Vol. 1. New York: John F. Rider.

6. Biewer, Matt. 1975. *The Designer's Guide to Programmed Logic for PLS 400 Systems*. PRO-LOG Corporation, 852 Airport Road, Monterey, Calif.

7. Osborne, Adam. 1975. *An Introduction to Microcomputers*. New York: McGraw-Hill.

8. *Science Digest Special,* Summer 1980. Hearst Corporation, 224 West 57th Street, New York, N.Y. 10019.

9. *TRS-80 Microcomputer News,* August 1980. Radio Shack's monthly newsletter published for TRS-80 owners.

10. Grove, Andrew S. 1980. Intel Takes Aim at the 80's. *Electronics*.

11. Luerhmann, Arthur. 1980. Computer Illiteracy—A National Crisis and a Solution for It. *Byte*, 5(7), pp. 98–102.

12. Papert, Seymour. 1980. New Cultures from New Technologies. *Byte*.

13. Weinberg, Victor. 1980. *Structured Analysis*. Englewood Cliffs, N.J.: Prentice-Hall.

14. Ogdin, Carol Anne. 1978. *Software Design for Microcomputers*. Englewood Cliffs, N.J.: Prentice-Hall.

The definitions marked "British" were suggested by Anthony Chandor's book, *The Penguin Dictionary of Microprocessors*, Penguin Books, 1981. The American translations are mine. There are other magazine articles, manufacturers' brochures, specifications, technical applications, notes, etc., too numerous to mention, and I am indeed grateful to their authors.